NEW EDITION

First Certificate

Practice Tests

Plus with Key

Nick Kenny

Lucrecia Luque-Mortimer

www.cv-library.co.uk
www.jobs.telegraph.co.uk
www.jobsite.co.uk
www.monster.co.uk
www.totaljobs.co.uk
www.theengineerjobs.co.uk
www.linkedin.com

TEACHING NOT JUST TESTING

PEARSON
Longman

with iTests

Exam Overview

The **First Certificate in English** is an intermediate level examination which is held three times a year in March, June and December. There are five papers in the exam and each paper receives an equal weighting of 20 percent of the marks. Papers are:

Paper 1 Reading   1 hour
Paper 2 Writing   1 hour 20 minutes
Paper 3 Use of English   45 minutes
Paper 4 Listening   40 minutes (approximately)
Paper 5 Speaking   14 minutes (for each pair of students)

- The examination questions are task-based and simulate real-life tasks.

- Questions in Papers 1–3 are text-based. This means that there is always something to read when doing the tasks.

- Rubrics are important and should be read carefully. They set the context and give important information about the tasks.

- For Papers 1, 3 and 4 you have to write your answers on a separate answer sheet.

Paper	Formats	Task focus
Reading Three tasks 30 reading comprehension questions	Part 1: answering multiple-choice questions. Part 2: choosing which sentence fits into gaps in a text. Part 3: deciding which of 4–6 short extracts or paragraphs contains given information or ideas.	Part 1: reading for detailed understanding of the text. Part 2: reading to understand text structure. Part 3: reading to locate specific information, detail, opinion and attitude.
Writing Two tasks	Part 1: compulsory task: using given information to write a letter or email of 120–150 words. Part 2: producing one piece of writing of 120–180 words, from a choice of five. Either an informal letter, a story, a report, an article or an essay.	Part 1: focus on content and organisation of input information for a given target audience. Part 2: focus on writing for a specific target reader, using appropriate layout and register.
Use of English Four tasks 42 questions 50 marks	Part 1: multiple-choice cloze. Choosing which word from a choice of 4 fits in each of 12 gaps in the text. Part 2: open cloze. Writing the missing word in each of 12 gaps in a text. Part 3: word formation. Choosing the form of the word given so that it fits into the gap in the text. Part 4: key-word transformations. Using the key word to complete a new sentence which means the same as the one given.	Part 1: choice of vocabulary and relationships between words. Part 2: grammar, vocabulary and knowledge of expressions. Part 3: grammatical accuracy and knowledge of vocabulary and expressions. Part 4: grammatical accuracy and knowledge of vocabulary and sentence structure.
Listening Four tasks 40 minutes 30 questions	Part 1: 8 short texts each with 1 multiple-choice question. Part 2: long text with 10 sentence-completion questions. Part 3: set of 5 short texts on a theme to match to 1 of 6 prompts. Part 4: long text with 7 multiple-choice questions.	Part 1: understanding gist, detail, function, purpose, attitude, etc. Part 2: locating and recording specific information. Part 3: understanding gist and main points. Part 4: understanding attitude, opinion, gist, main ideas and specific information.
Speaking Four tasks 14 minutes per pair of candidates	Part 1: examiner-led conversation. Part 2: individual long turn with visual and written prompts. Part 3: two-way collaborative task with visual and written prompts. Part 4: three-way interlocutor-led discussion.	Part 1: giving personal information. Part 2: organising discourse, describing, comparing, giving opinions. Part 3: sustaining interaction, expressing, justifying and eliciting ideas, agreeing and disagreeing. Part 4: expressing and justifying ideas, agreeing and disagreeing.

Contents

TEST 1: READING

Part 1

You are going to read a magazine article about a rally driver. For questions **1–8**, choose the answer (**A**, **B**, **C** or **D**) which you think fits best according to the text.

Driving in the desert

My family are farmers in France, and by the age of ten, I could manoeuvre a tractor into a field to pick up straw bales. For my driving test, I learned how to reverse into a parking space by practising between two tractors.

I'm the extraterrestrial of the family: I've always needed to prove that I can adapt to new situations. I'd never left France until 1998 – and then I went to Australia, the most distant country possible. I worked on a sheep farm there, driving a 4x4 all the time, and spent four months driving around the country on my own. That was when I first came into contact with the desert, and I wanted to return to it.

But it was my competitive spirit that drew me to the all-female Gazelles Rally in the Moroccan desert. I did it to see if I could survive in the desert and not be afraid. Taking part in the rally involves spending eight days in the desert, including two sets of two-day marathons when you're on your own overnight with your team-mate. The rally will push you to the limits of your physical and mental capacity, so it's very important to choose the right team-mate, to make sure you have the same goal and the same way of working. But the key thing is for you both to keep your courage and remain confident.

Participants – known as the *gazelles* – drive 4x4s, quad bikes, motorbikes or trucks, and use a compass and a map to navigate their way to marker flags that have been planted in the desert – always in places that are really difficult to get at. You have to drive up and down huge sand dunes, the highest of which are about twenty metres. Every morning at base camp you have to prepare your maps, by marking the position of the day's flags. Then you have to plan the best route to them. It takes time to learn how to do
40 this, how to understand the landscape, because you are all alone in the emptiness – there are no landmarks, it is all just flat. On our first day, my team-mate and I felt quite frightened by it

– we thought we'd get lost. So we decided to drive in a straight line for half an hour in search of geographical features. Then we found some mountains.

It rained a lot during the rally, and the thing that scared us most was the thought of not being able to get out of the mud. Some women were stuck for about twelve hours overnight before the mud dried. My team-mate and I managed to get through, though, because we set off first, when the ground was less damaged. Each vehicle carries a satellite tracking system with it, and every half-hour the rally organisers use this to check on you: if a car isn't moving, they go to the rescue. Once, we were all alone in our tent in a storm, and feeling a bit scared. An official rally vehicle came and reassured us that we wouldn't be washed away.

I had great difficulty finding a sponsor – it costs about €6000 to hire a vehicle and €14,000 to participate in the rally, plus you have to hire safety equipment. It's always the people you least expect who help you most. The big dealers for four-wheel-drive vehicles refused to finance
68 what they called 'a girls' jaunt in the desert'. It was a small, independent garage that provided us with an 11-year-old 4x4 for nothing – and we didn't have a single breakdown.

Speed is not a factor in this competition. Men have a tendency to drive a bit faster than women. They're so sure they've chosen the right route that they're less good at anticipating problems. A man who was doing a television programme on the rally refused to believe that it was difficult or that women could sometimes be better than him.

I want to do the rally again next year. Taking part in it puts life's problems into perspective, and it's also a big thing on my CV: it shows people I can see a project through. When I meet the top people in my company now, I feel far more self-assured.

Tip Strip
- The questions follow the order of the text.
- Read the text carefully. Don't worry if you don't understand every word.
- Try to find your own answer to the questions before you look at options **A**, **B**, **C** and **D**.
- <u>Underline key words</u> in the question then find the part of the text where the answer is and underline words there.
- Find the option which best answers the question according to what you have found in the text.

Question 1: Read the text carefully. What did she know before she went and what did she discover when she got there?

Question 2: What does the text say about 'choosing the right team-mate'. Read what follows to find the answer.

Question 3: Look before the pronoun to find out what it took time to learn.

Question 4: Look for another way of saying 'greatest fear' in the text.

Question 5: Read carefully about the writer's vehicle.

1 Why did the writer go to Australia?

    A to further develop her driving skills
    B to get practice in driving in desert conditions
    C to visit members of her family who farmed there
    D to experience living in an unfamiliar environment

2 In the writer's opinion, the ideal rallying team-mate is someone who

    A will keep you from feeling afraid at night.
    B can make up for any weaknesses you have.
    C does not take the competition too seriously.
    D will share your general aims and attitudes.

3 What does the word 'this' in line 40 refer to?

    A driving in difficult places
    B finding important landmarks
    C deciding which route to take
    D drawing flags on a map

4 The writer's greatest fear in the desert was that she might

    A lose her way in bad weather.
    B become stuck in wet ground.
    C damage her vehicle in the mud.
    D have to be rescued by other competitors.

5 What does the writer say about the cost of the rally?

    A Hiring a vehicle was her biggest expense.
    B Safety equipment was provided by the organisers.
    C She was surprised that a small garage sponsored her.
    D A new vehicle would have reduced her maintenance bill.

6 By using the phrase 'a girls' jaunt' (line 68), the big dealers showed that they felt

    A unimpressed by the writer's driving skills.
    B a lack of respect for this particular event.
    C sure that the writer wouldn't complete the rally.
    D an unwillingness to sponsor rallying in general.

7 According to the writer, men rally drivers

    A fail to realise when something is about to go wrong.
    B tend to feel overconfident when driving at speed.
    C seem to have fewer problems with navigation.
    D refuse to accept the advice of women.

8 In the last paragraph, the writer suggests that taking part in the rally

    A has improved her career prospects.
    B has impressed her superiors at work.
    C is something that she will do every year.
    D is creating certain problems in her private life.

You are going to read an article about the music used in gyms. Seven sentences have been removed from the article. Choose from the sentences **A–H** the one which fits each gap (**9–15**). There is one extra sentence which you do not need to use.

Music to get fit by

An aerobics teacher argues that music can increase our workout productivity

At college, I used to go to the gym regularly but I never liked the music they played in the classes. I trained as an instructor largely so that I could have control of the stereo. Now I teach twenty hours of aerobic classes a week and so I always associate physical activity with banging house music at 140 beats per minute.

This is not as crazy as you might think. Music and exercise have long been known to be close companions. **9** [ ] He is also the architect of the Brunel Music Rating Inventory (BMRI), designed to rate the motivational qualities of music.

Karageorghis says we have an underlying predisposition to react to musical stimuli. 'Music is beneficial,' he explains, 'because of the similarities between rhythm and human movement. The synchronisation of music with exercise consistently demonstrates increased levels of work output among exercise participants.' **10** [ ]

For James Cracknell, the rower, the ideal music was a Red Hot Chili Peppers' album, which he says played an integral part in his preparation and, ultimately, his Olympic victory. **11** [ ] If you are not familiar with this word, it means that during repetitive exercise, music essentially diverts attention away from the sensation of fatigue. The right music can almost persuade your body that you are in fact having a nice sit down and a coffee.

Not everyone, however, shares the same taste in tunes. 'Can you turn that racket down?' said a participant in one of my classes before storming out. Reaching a consensus on music is notoriously tricky – which makes communal exercise classes problematic. There are, however, some rules that professional fitness instructors follow. **12** [ ]

Most importantly, however, the music should mirror your heartbeat. The instructor should choose the music to go with the different phases of a class, from the warm up, to high intensity, to the final relaxing phase. It's advisable to follow this sequence when you work out alone, too, and not make the mistake a good friend of mine made. **13** [ ]

Instructors and gyms often buy ready-mixed CDs that come with a music licence, without which they can be fined heavily. A frequent complaint by those who go to classes is that they hear the same old songs over and over again. **14** [ ] It is also true, sadly, that most people respond best in motivational terms to quite awful songs – music they wouldn't necessarily be proud to have on their iPod.

15 [ ] In order to prepare mentally, for example, golfers can get hold of a special range of music just for them. Whatever your sport, I'd like to give you some final words of advice. As Karageorghis suggests, enjoy the beat and let the music motivate you, but never forget your main objective is to exercise and music is only there to help you do that.

Tip Strip
- Read through the base text for general understanding.
- Read the text around each gap carefully.
- Read the sentences and find one that fits in with the meaning of each part. Check for topic and language links before and after the sentence.
- Read the paragraph again to check that it makes a complete sentence with your answer in place.

Question 9: The sentence before the gap describes music and exercise as 'close companions'. Which sentence refers to the relationship between music and exercise?

Question 11: The gap is followed by 'not familiar with this word'. Can you find a word that needs explaining in the sentences?

Question 12: The sentence before the gap mentions 'some rules'. Can you find a sentence that gives an example of a rule?

Question 13: Do you need to find a sentence that describes the mistake that was made?

A But perhaps the most useful thing about music is that it allows even the humble gym-goer or runner to practise a technique used by elite athletes, known as 'disassociation'.

B These days you can find music tailored to suit an incredibly diverse range of sports and exercise needs.

C One of them is that the music must be appropriate to the type of class and not just the instructor's personal enthusiasm for a particular genre or artist.

D This is mostly because only a limited number of them are released for public performance each year, and partly because teachers universally favour the most popular tracks.

E The most convenient is the gym called *Third Space* in London's Soho, which does several sessions a week to live DJ accompaniment.

F He was cooling down to techno music, which left him feeling nervous and twitchy all day.

G Choose the right music and, according to Karageorghis, you can up your workout productivity by as much as twenty percent.

H Dr Costas Karageorghis, a sports and exercise psychologist who is also a musician, has spent more than a decade studying the link between athletic activity and music.

You are going to read a magazine article about five people who each write a personal blog. For questions **16–30**, choose from the people (**A–E**). The people may be chosen more than once.

A	**Ann Handley**
B	**Dave Armano**
C	**Carol Krishner**
D	**Debbie Weil**
E	**Tristan Hussey**

Which person

started writing the blog as a way of improving career prospects? **16**

says they use the personal blog in professional activities? **17**

warns prospective bloggers about a loss of privacy? **18**

mentions having certain difficulties as a teenager? **19**

made a decision to improve the quality of the blog? **20**

is not concerned about making errors in the blog? **21**

felt no need to learn anything new before starting to write blogs? **22**

believes that blogging has improved their language skills? **23**

initially lacked confidence in their ability to attract readers to the blog? **24**

was surprised by the response to the blog? **25** **26**

compares the ease of writing blogs to other types of writing? **27**

values the fact that the blog provides a break from work? **28**

remembers other people being less open about what they had written? **29**

has offered other new bloggers help in starting their blogs? **30**

Ann Handley Like many of my school friends, I used to spend hours every day writing a diary. But while they kept them hidden under their beds, I needed an audience, interaction and feedback. One day, my teacher encouraged me to join a pen friend organisation and I used to write pages of fascinating detail about my teacher, my friends, my dog … I even invented a few personalities, the details of which were far more interesting than my own life. So when one of my colleagues explained to me what blogging was all about – the frequent postings, the feedback, the trackbacks – I felt confident that I already knew all about it. I am now a marketing specialist and my blog is a business tool. But at the same time I am reliving the joy of communicating and the thrill of the conversation.

Why do people start writing blogs? Read the personal stories of five bloggers

Dave Armano A year ago I was a professional minding my own business. When I started reading blogs, I would say to myself: 'There's so much information out there – so many smart people.' I decided to start my own blog, but I had no idea what I was doing. I was basically a nobody and I was trying to get people to listen to me. What was I thinking? But then I created a visual for my blog and before I knew it, I had all these other blogs linking to me – doing weird stuff like trackbacks. I had no idea what a trackback was, but I went from forty hits a day to close to a hundred overnight. It was amazing! That's when I stopped to think: if I wanted traffic, I needed to get some good content there, and that's what really worked for me.

Carol Krishner It's great to have my personal blog because I feel free and if I make mistakes I learn from the experience. I'm a lecturer, and it's refreshing to be able to step outside my academic interests and into a different world. But it's interesting that when you choose topics to write about you give others hints about yourself, and people do get to know you. So it's not the thing to do if you want to remain anonymous. One of the first lessons I learnt is that the blogosphere is a genuine community. After asking a question in a blog comment about what qualities are needed in a good blog, I soon got spot-on advice from a blogger I didn't even know. Then I had an invitation to a local face-to-face blogger meet-up, which was an amazing experience.

Debbie Weil I started my first blog exactly three years ago for a very practical reason. It was clear to me that blogs were going to become a useful tool in my future job as a journalist. I needed to know how to use this new tool, and I figured blogging myself was the quickest way to get up to speed. I learnt quickly and since then I've helped others launch their own personal blogs. The simplicity of blogging software enables me to write short entries without any problems or delays. Writing a 750-word article is a daunting task, but a quick blog entry takes less than a minute. And yet the effect is so significant – I get calls from companies saying they've read my blog and would I be available to give a presentation, for a large fee.

Tristan Hussey Writing has been a struggle for me for most of my academic life. In my first high school year I had serious spelling problems all the time. At college, thanks to a spell checker and some practice, I did fine. In 2004, I was in an administrative job and feeling that I was only using a small portion of my skills. I had heard about this blogging thing and decided I should give it a go. I wrote one blog but deleted it after a couple of days. Then I realised that if I wanted a better job, I'd need to get good at this. So I started reading blogs, writing blogs – it was a daily ritual of reading and writing. And guess what, my writing was getting better, and, incredibly, I got noticed by employers. Today I work for a blog software company.

Part 1

You **must** answer this question. Write your answer in **120–150** words in an appropriate style.

1   You have received an email from Jennie, an English-speaking friend who has recently moved to your country and now lives near you. Read Jennie's email and the notes you have made. Then write an email to Jennie, using **all** your notes.

---

email   Page 1 of 1

From: Jennie Sullivan
Sent: 20th July 2008
Subject: Getting fit

I have decided to try and get fitter, but I am finding it difficult to decide what to do. There's a park near here, can you join me to go running in the mornings?   → No, because …

As you know, I'm a bit lazy, so I need to go to a gym because I would never do any exercise at home. Are there any good gyms in this area?   ← Yes, give details

I'm really busy with my schoolwork. Do you think I can get enough exercise if I go just twice a week to the gym?   → Yes, if you …

I know you're a very good swimmer. I'd like to learn how to swim really well. Can you teach me?   ← Yes, say when and where

Now I must go to buy sports clothes and equipment.

See you soon.

Love,

Jennie

Write your **email**. You must use grammatically correct sentences with accurate spelling and punctuation in a style appropriate to the situation.

Tip Strip
- You don't have to be imaginative. Read the instructions carefully and underline key words, e.g. <u>recently moved to your country</u> or <u>using all your notes</u>.
- Read the email. What information does your friend ask for and what notes have you made? Your email must include all the points in the notes.
- Think about who you are writing to. What style has your friend used, formal or informal? Use the same style in your answer.
- Plan your answer. In paragraph 1, you may want to answer your friend's first and second questions (why you cannot join her, and what good gyms you know). In paragraph 2, you can answer the next two questions (explaining what she must do if she goes to the gym only twice a week, and suggesting a day/time and a place where you can teach her to swim). Remember you must always use the notes for your answers.
- Remember, your email must have opening and closing lines.
- You have to write words and sentences in full – the style used for 'texting' is not acceptable in Cambridge exams.
- When you've finished, read through the input information again. Have you included everything?
- Check the word limit, but don't waste time counting every word.
- Check your grammar and spelling.

Tip Strip

Write an answer to **one** of the questions **2–4** in this part. Write an answer in **120–180** words in an appropriate style.

2 You have seen an announcement in an international magazine.

> **When I was really small**
>
> Tell us about your best friend when you were a child and say why you got on well together.
>
> The best article will win a book as a prize.

Write your **article**.

3 You recently saw this notice in your local newspaper.

> **Write a review for us!**
>
> Have you visited a museum lately? If so, could you write a review of your visit for the college magazine? Include information about the exhibits, the information available and the facilities, and say whether you would recommend it to other students.
>
> The best reviews will receive a book token as a prize.

Write your **review.**

4 Your teacher has asked you to write a story for an international magazine. The story must **begin** with the following words:

As soon as Roy opened the door, he knew something was wrong.

Write your **story.**

5 Answer **one** of the following two questions based on your reading of **one** of these set books.

(a) Author – *Name of book*
Compare the main character as s/he is at the beginning and at the end of the story. Write an **essay** saying in what ways s/he has changed as a result of events.

(b) Author – *Name of book*

> *I have just seen the film [name of book] and I really liked it. I know you have read the book. Do you think it is worth reading or will I be bored? Jack*

Write a **letter** to Jack answering his question and giving reasons for your opinions.

Tip Strip

- Read the questions carefully. Choose a question you have ideas and vocabulary for.
- Underline key points in the question and use them in your answer.
- Before you start writing, think of the task type you have chosen. Is it a story, an article, a report, a letter, an essay (composition) or a review? Remember what you learnt about writing each task type.
- Before you start writing, note the main point you want to include in each paragraph.
- Pay attention to organisation: all options require you to write in paragraphs.
- Re-read what you have written and check for spelling and grammar mistakes.

Question 2:
- Introduce your topic in the first paragraph and summarise what you have said in the last paragraph.
- You are asked to describe your friend and explain why you got on well together. Use vocabulary related to childhood activities, feelings and memories, and the language of description, opinion and explanation.
- Try to use varied language and avoid repeating adjectives, e.g. 'nice', 'good'.

Question 3:
- Use vocabulary related to items, information and facilities you may find in a museum. Jot down some of this vocabulary so you do not forget to use it.

Question 4:
- Think of how your story will develop before you start writing. How will the story end?
- Check your verb sequences, e.g. simple past / past perfect.

Tip Strip
- Read the text for general understanding first.
- Only one of the options, **A, B, C** or **D** fits the gap.
- The option you choose must fit the context of the text as a whole.
- Check the words before and after the gap. For example, some words can only be used with certain prepositions, and some words are part of set phrases or phrasal verbs.
- When you have finished the task, read through the text again and make sure that the text makes complete sense with your answers in place.

Question 1: This is a common expression. Which word sounds best coming after 'out and'?

Question 4: This is a fixed phrase. Which of the options will make a phrase that describes a quantity?

Question: 5: Which of these words is usually followed by the preposition 'on'?

Question 7: Which of these words usually describes sunshine?

Question 10: Which of these words is usually used after weather?

Part 1

For questions **1–12**, read the text below and decide which answer (**A, B, C** or **D**) best fits each gap. There is an example at the beginning **(0)**.

In the exam you mark your answers on a separate answer sheet.

Example:

0 A open   **B** free   **C** clear   **D** wide

0	A	B	C	D
	—	▭	▭	▭

Don't forget your hat

An important point to remember if you like spending time out in the **(0)** ...... air is that the human head doesn't work very well outdoors if it becomes too hot, cold or wet. That's why a hat is a good investment, wherever you're planning to go out and **(1)** .... Surprisingly, a single waterproof hat with a brim will do the **(2)** ...... adequately in most conditions

In cold climates, the problem is that the head is **(3)** ...... heat all the time. As **(4)** ...... as fifty to sixty percent of your body's heat is lost through the head and neck, **(5)** ...... on which scientist you believe. Clearly this heat loss needs to be prevented, but it's important to remember that hats don't actually **(6)** ...... you warm, they simply stop heat escaping.

Just as important is the need to protect your neck from the effects of **(7)** ...... sunlight, and the brim of your hat will do this. If you prefer a baseball cap, **(8)** ...... buying one that has a drop down 'tail' at the back to stop your neck **(9)** ...... sunburnt.

And in wet weather **(10)** ...... , hats are often more practical than pulling up the hood of your waterproof coat because when you **(11)** ...... your head, the hat goes with you, **(12)** ...... the hood usually does not.

0	**A**	open	**B**	free	**C**	clear	**D**	wide
1	**A**	around	**B**	about	**C**	along	**D**	above
2	**A**	job	**B**	task	**C**	role	**D**	duty
3	**A**	giving away	**B**	sending out	**C**	dropping off	**D**	running down
4	**A**	soon	**B**	long	**C**	well	**D**	much
5	**A**	according	**B**	regarding	**C**	depending	**D**	relating
6	**A**	maintain	**B**	stay	**C**	hold	**D**	keep
7	**A**	sharp	**B**	keen	**C**	bright	**D**	deep
8	**A**	consider	**B**	recommend	**C**	advise	**D**	suggest
9	**A**	suffering	**B**	going	**C**	having	**D**	getting
10	**A**	occasions	**B**	positions	**C**	cases	**D**	conditions
11	**A**	alter	**B**	switch	**C**	turn	**D**	spin
12	**A**	instead of	**B**	whereas	**C**	rather than	**D**	thereby

Tip Strip

- Read the text for general understanding.
- Most of the gaps can be filled by grammatical words, not topic vocabulary.
- Decide which type of word each gap needs, e.g. preposition, relative pronoun, conjunction, verb, adverb, etc.
- Look out for fixed expressions, dependent prepositions after certain words, and linking words and phrases.
- The word you choose must make sense in the context of the text as a whole. So when you've finished the task, read through and check that the text makes complete sense with your answers in place.

Question 14: Which relative pronoun is needed here?

Question 17: Which linking word is needed here?

Question 22: Which is the correct preposition to complete the expression?

Question 23: A verb form is needed to complete the passive form. Which tense will it be in?

Part 2

For questions **13–24**, read the text below and think of the word which best fits each gap. Use only **one** word in each gap. There is an example at the beginning **(0)**.

In the exam you write your answers IN CAPITAL LETTERS on a separate answer sheet.

Example: | 0 | W | I | T | H | | | | | | | |

Penguins on the move

For years, the penguins at San Francisco Zoo were happy **(0)** ...... their lives. They used to go for the occasional swim during the summer, but spent the winter resting in their burrows – only coming **(13)** ...... at mealtimes when fish was provided for them.

Then one day, six new penguins, **(14)** ...... had been entertaining the visitors at a theme park in San Diego, arrived to share the pool. These new arrivals immediately dived in to show off their swimming skills. Ever **(15)** ...... that moment the pool has been alive with fifty-two birds swimming around nonstop, **(16)** ...... if they were going on a long journey.

'**(17)** ...... I know a lot about penguins,' said one zookeeper, 'I don't know **(18)** ...... to explain this. It's **(19)** ...... watching fifty-two tuxedos going round in a washing machine!'

Scientists, **(20)** ...... , think they may have the answer. Apparently, penguins are very social and inquisitive birds, and **(21)** ...... new individuals join a group, they always create a lot of interest.

In the wild, penguins of this type typically swim thousands of miles each year **(22)** ...... search of food, and it **(23)** ...... thought that the behaviour of the newcomers may **(24)** ...... reawakened the migratory instinct in the San Francisco birds. This has certainly made them firm favourites with visitors to the zoo.

Tip Strip

- Read the text for general understanding.
- Decide which type of word is needed for each gap (noun, adjective, etc).
- Look at the whole sentence, not just the line including the gap.
- Look at the word in capitals to the right of the gap. You may need to add a prefix or a suffix or make other changes to this word.
- Check the meaning of the text to see if the word is singular or plural.
- The word you choose must make sense in the context of the text as a whole. So when you've finished the task, read through and check that the text makes complete sense with your answers in place.
- Check your spelling.

Question 25: Is a noun or an adjective needed here?

Question 27: Will this word be positive or negative? How do you know?

Question 29: What is the noun made from this adjective? Be careful of your spelling.

Question 30: Two changes are needed, a prefix and a suffix, to make this a negative adjective.

Question 31: This word needs a suffix. Both negative and positive suffixes exist; which do you need here?

Question 34: How does the end of this adjective change when it becomes a noun?

For questions **25–34**, read the text below. Use the word given in capitals at the end of some of the lines to form a word that fits the gap **in the same line**. There is an example at the beginning **(0)**.

In the exam you write your answers IN CAPITAL LETTERS on a separate answer sheet.

Example: | 0 | F | A | S | C | I | N | A | T | I | O | N |

The sky at night

For anyone with a **(0)** …… for the study of the night sky, **FASCINATE**

Hawaii is one of the best places in the world to get a clear view

of the stars and planets. This is because of the island's geographical

setting. Because it is a **(25)** …… area, situated in the middle of **MOUNTAIN**

a large expanse of ocean, Hawaii is much less affected by light

(26) …… than most other parts of the world. **POLLUTE**

If you are **(27)** …… enough to go to the top of the dormant volcano **FORTUNE**

known as Mauna Kea, the view is even more **(28)** ……. . The **IMPRESS**

volcano, which rises to a **(29)** …… of 4205 metres is one of the **HIGH**

best places in the world to get **(30)** …… views of the night sky **INTERRUPT**

and therefore is the location for more than a dozen of the

world's finest telescopes.

Of special significance is the WM Keck Observatory where there

are a pair of extremely large and **(31)** …… telescopes. In recent **POWER**

years these telescopes have been responsible for the **(32)** …… **DISCOVER**

of around forty new planets beyond our solar system. By proving

the **(33)** …… of these planets, astronomers have increased the **EXIST**

(34) …… that one day another inhabited planet like our own **PROBABLE**

will be found.

Tip Strip

- Look at the key word. What type of word is it? What usually follows it, e.g. an infinitive, a gerund, a pronoun, a preposition, another verb, or is it part of a set phrase or phrasal verb?
- Think about other words that need to change in the new word order, e.g. an adjective may become a noun, or vice versa.
- Write your answer on the question paper and read both sentences again.
- Make sure that you haven't added any extra information.
- Make sure you haven't changed the meaning.
- Then, write only the missing words on the answer sheet.
- Check your spelling.
- Remember that contracted words count as two words, e.g. 'don't' = 'do not'.

Question 35: Which verb comes here? Remember to keep the tense the same.

Question 36: A passive verb form is needed. Remember to keep the tense the same.

Question 37: Which common expression about the future uses the word 'forward'?

Question 38: A noun is needed after 'my'.

Question 39: You need to make the key word negative in your answer.

Question 40: Is the key word followed by a gerund or an infinitive?

For questions **35–42**, complete the second sentence so that it has a similar meaning to the first sentence, using the word given. **Do not change the word given.** You must use between **two** and **five** words, including the word given. Here is an example **(0)**.

Example:

0   What type of music do you like best?

FAVOURITE

What .... type of music?

The gap can be filled by the words 'is your favourite', so you write:

Example: | **0** | IS YOUR FAVOURITE |

In the exam you write only the missing words IN CAPITAL LETTERS on a separate answer sheet.

---

35   How much does a new laptop computer cost?

PRICE

What .... of a new laptop computer?

36   They are opening a new branch of that bookshop in our town.

BEING

A new branch of that bookshop .... in our town.

37   Patrick can't wait to see the team's next home game.

FORWARD

Patrick is really .... the team's next home game.

38   Denise said that she'd always intended to invite Phil to the party.

MY

'It had always .... invite Phil to the party,' said Denise.

39 Paolo damaged his brother's digital camera by accident.

MEAN

Paolo ……………… his brother's digital camera.

40 Suzy says she will only play tennis if Fiona plays with her.

UNLESS

Suzy has refused ……………… plays with her.

41 People think that the famous actress will arrive in the city this morning.

EXPECTED

The famous actress …………….. in the city this morning.

42 Canoeing was the activity which excited Ralph most.

FOUND

The activity ……………… was canoeing.

Part 1

You will hear people talking in eight different situations. For questions **1–8**, choose the best answer (**A**, **B** or **C**).

Tip Strip

- Each question is based on a different listening text with a separate mark.
- You hear each text twice before you hear the next text.
- Relax and concentrate on each new text. Don't worry about the one that you've just done.
- Look at the first sentence in each question. It gives you information about what you are going to hear.
- Read the question and underline key words. Make sure you know what you are listening for. Listen for the answer to the question.
- Choose the option which is closest to what you have understood.
- The second time you listen, check to make sure you're correct.
- If you're not sure, guess. You may have understood more than you think.
- Don't listen for single words. Listen for the general meaning of what you hear.
- Don't worry if you hear words that you don't know.

Question 1: The listening text mentions a tourist attraction (castle) and facilities (showers), but these are not why she recommends the campsite.

Question 2: You are listening for the girl's opinion, but the boy's response to what she says will also help you to get the answer.

Question 4: Think about the question. What are you listening for? The word 'call' comes at the end of the listening text, but you need to understand what comes before to answer the question.

1   You overhear a woman recommending a campsite.

Why does she recommend it?

A   It's close to tourist attractions.

B   It's in an area of natural beauty.

C   It has a wide range of facilities.

[ ] 1

2   You overhear two friends talking about global warming.

How does the girl feel about it?

A   pessimistic about the future

B   surprised at the effects it's having

C   unconvinced that there's a problem

[ ] 2

3   You overhear a young couple talking about moving to the country.

Why does the man object to the idea?

A   He wouldn't be able to work there.

B   He'd miss the facilities of the city.

C   He wouldn't be near to his friends.

[ ] 3

4   You hear a part of a radio programme about food.

Why should listeners call the programme?

A   to take part in a recipe competition

B   to find out about a cookery course

C   to ask questions about cooking

[ ] 4

5 You hear the beginning of a programme about college canteens.

What point is being made about them?

A The choice of food has improved.

B Students like the food on offer there.

C Teachers complain about the quality of the food.

	5

Question 6: Be careful! The last thing she talks about is money (income), but is this the answer to the question?

6 You hear a young woman talking about her career.

Why did she accept a job in a bookshop?

A She needed a steady income.

B She thought it would be enjoyable.

C She hoped to improve certain skills.

	6

7 You hear part of a programme about a clothes designer.

What does the woman like about the clothes he designs?

A They are practical.

B They are colourful.

C They are original.

	7

8 You overhear a discussion about the sport of snow-kiting.

What does the man say about it?

A It's easier to learn than other winter sports.

B It's more dangerous than other winter sports.

C It requires less equipment than other winter sports.

	8

You will hear a radio programme about a boy called Michael who crossed the Atlantic in a sailing boat. For questions **9–18**, complete the sentences.

Sailing solo across the Atlantic

To achieve his record, Michael had to sail a total of

[_____ 9] kilometres without any help.

Michael helped to design his boat which was called

[_____ 10]

Michael and his father were concerned in case any

[_____ 11] came too close to them.

All the food that Michael took on his voyage was in

[_____ 12] bought at the supermarket.

The type of food which Michael missed most on the trip was

[_____ 13]

Michael enjoyed using his [_____ 14]

to keep track of what his father was doing.

Michael's favourite pastimes on the boat were using his sister's

[_____ 15] and reading.

Michael got a fright when a

[_____ 16] landed on him.

The name of the charity that Michael is raising funds for is

[_____ 17]

When Michael sails round the world, he plans to take

[_____ 18] with him in case he feels homesick.

Tip Strip

- There are five different speakers talking on a different topic. You hear all five once, then all five repeated.
- Before you listen, read the instructions carefully. What are the people talking about? What are you listening for?
- Then, read options **A** to **F** so that you're ready to choose one as you listen to each speaker.
- If you're unsure about an answer, wait for the second listening before making a final decision.
- The first time you listen, pay attention to the speaker's main idea. Mark the option closest to this idea.
- The second time you listen, check your answers. You may need to change some of them.
- Sometimes a word in an option occurs in several extracts, for example:

  A: 'enthusiasm' is mentioned by speakers 2 and 4, but neither refers to renewing the speaker's enthusiasm.

  B: speaker 4 mentions 'equipment', but does not say it is the latest.

  E: All speakers mention learning new skills, but which speaker is unhappy not to have learnt them earlier in life?

  F: 'ingredients' are mentioned by speakers 1 and 5, but neither talks about searching for them.

You will hear five different people talking about cookery courses. For questions **19–23**, choose from the list (**A–F**) what each speaker says about the course they took. Use the letters only once. There is one extra letter which you do not need to use.

A   It helped me to renew my enthusiasm for cooking.

Speaker 1 [   ] **19**

B   It taught me how to use the latest kitchen equipment.

Speaker 2 [   ] **20**

C   It took into account the fact that I wasn't a beginner.

Speaker 3 [   ] **21**

D   It required me to do things rather than just watch.

Speaker 4 [   ] **22**

E   It gave me skills I wish I'd acquired earlier in life.

Speaker 5 [   ] **23**

F   It included an unexpected search for ingredients.

Tip Strip

- The questions follow the order of the text.
- Before you listen, read through the questions and underline key words.
- Listen to find the answer to the question, then choose the option (**A**, **B** or **C**) which is closest.
- The words in the options will be different from the words you hear.
- Most questions will be about people's ideas, opinions, feelings, etc.

Question 24: Pamela went to a shop, but did she work there? Pamela went to college, but when did she decide to become a designer? Listen for another way of saying 'decided'.

Question 26: Read the question. Remember you're listening for what Pamela thinks is 'most important'.

Question 27: The interviewer uses the word 'inspiration'. Listen to what Pamela says after this to find the answer.

Question 29: What does 'according to Pamela' mean?

Question 30: Listen to the whole of Pamela's last turn. What is her main message?

You will hear an interview with Pamela Green, a young fashion designer. For questions **24–30**, choose the best answer (**A**, **B** or **C**).

24 What helped Pamela to decide to become a fashion designer?

  A working as an assistant in a fashion shop
  B doing research into the fashion industry
  C attending a course on fashion design

  `24`

25 What does Pamela say about having a degree in fashion?

  A It's essential for promotion.
  B It's evidence of your ability.
  C It guarantees you a better income.

  `25`

26 Pamela says that when starting your own fashion label, it's most important to

  A enjoy the creative process.
  B contact shops that might sell it.
  C have a business plan.

  `26`

27 Where does Pamela usually find inspiration for her fashion designs?

  A in the work of other designers
  B in the styles of other countries
  C in the clothes her friends wear

  `27`

28 What aspect of her work does Pamela find most difficult to deal with?

  A the pressure to meet deadlines
  B the failure of some of her designs
  C the need to attend fashion shows

  `28`

29 According to Pamela, successful designers need to be able to

  A predict future fashions.
  B recognise all past styles.
  C get their designs published.

  `29`

30 What advice does Pamela have for people who want a career in fashion?

  A Be aware of the options available.
  B Don't be afraid of sudden fame.
  C Learn from your own errors.

  `30`

Tip Strip

Part 1

- The examiner will ask you questions in turn. Don't try to learn a little speech about yourself. This will not answer the examiner's questions properly.

Part 2

- A minute is quite a long time to talk. Don't panic, don't go too fast.
- Don't interrupt your partner's turn. Listen so you can comment afterwards.
- Don't give separate descriptions of each picture. Compare and contrast them from the beginning.
- If you don't know a word in one of the pictures, describe what you mean using other words.

Part 3

- Ask your partner for his/her opinions, don't just say what you think.
- You have to talk for three minutes, so don't decide or agree too soon – talk about all the pictures first.
- You don't have to agree with your partner.

Part 4

- The examiner may ask you questions in turn or may ask general questions for you both to answer.
- You don't have to agree with your partner, but try not to interrupt; let your partner finish, then say what you think.

Part 1 (3 minutes)

The examiner will ask you both to talk briefly about yourselves by answering questions such as:

> First of all, we'd like to know something about you.
> Where are you from? What do you like about living in …… ?
> What is there for young people to do in your area?

Part 2 (3 or 4 minutes)

You will each be asked to talk for a minute without interruption. You will each have two different photographs to talk about. You will also have to answer a question after your partner has spoken.

Study places (compare, contrast and speculate)

Turn to pictures 1 and 2 on page 124, which show people studying.

Candidate A, compare and contrast these photographs, and say why the people have chosen these places to study. You have a minute to do this.

Candidate B, do you ever study in a library?

Doing exercise (compare, contrast and speculate)

Turn to pictures 1 and 2 on page 125, which show people exercising.

Candidate B, compare and contrast these photographs, and say how good these forms of exercise might be for the people in the photos. You have a minute to do this.

Candidate A, do you like team sports?

Part 3 (3 or 4 minutes)

You will be asked to discuss something together without interruption by the examiner. You will have a page of pictures to help you.

Travel problems (discuss and evaluate)

Turn to the pictures on page 126, which show different problems people may have when they travel (go on holiday).

How serious are these problems for the people involved?

What can people do to avoid these problems?

Part 4 (3 or 4 minutes)

The examiner encourages you to develop the discussion in Part 3 by asking questions such as:

> Do you like 'adventure' holidays? Why/Why not?
> Has anything like this ever happened to you? How did you react?
> How dangerous is it to go on safari holidays?

TEST 2: READING

Part 1

You are going to read an extract from a novel. For questions **1–8**, choose the answer (**A**, **B**, **C** or **D**) which you think fits best according to the text.

There was a book with bed-and-breakfast places in it amongst the guidebooks and maps on the back seat of my aunt's car and we found somewhere to stay in there. It was a big, old farmhouse down the end of a track, in a dip. There were three cows in the nearest field, sheep up on a ridge, hens in the yard, a few sheds and barns standing around, and a rosy-cheeked farmer's wife. After a day driving round, I was really impressed with the place initially, thinking we'd finally found the true countryside. Now my aunt could write whatever she was supposed to write about it, and we could both relax and go home.

But when I suggested that, she just said she wasn't expected to write about accommodation. Then, when we got talking to the woman, the place wasn't quite what it seemed anyway. The only field that went with the farmhouse was the one beside the track, with the cows in it, the rest belonged to a farm over the hill. The barns were rented to another farmer and the woman came from the city and was married to a travelling salesman. From close to, you could see the colour in her cheeks came out of a jar marked 'blusher'. The hens were hers, though. She'd been a professional bed-and-breakfast lady for three years, she said, and this was the worst season ever, and, yes, we could have separate rooms, two of each if we liked.

Perhaps she and her husband spent all their money on winter holidays, or perhaps they just didn't have any, but they certainly didn't spend a lot on the house. The bedrooms were huge and they hardly had any furniture in them – just a double bed in each, one of those wardrobes with hangers on one side and shelves down the other, and a wooden chair. There was a dangling light cord over each bed, which worked the centre light, but no bedside lamp.

I could tell that my aunt wasn't knocked out by it because she whispered to me, 'All very clean, isn't it?' which is what Mum says about a place when she can't find anything else good. 'Well there isn't much to get dirty,' I whispered back. But the woman, Mrs Vosper, obviously assumed we'd stay, so we did. She asked if we were on holiday, and I listened with interest to my aunt's answer. I don't think I really understood at that point what she was doing, and it had got a bit late to ask her myself. I was supposed to know. But all she said was: 'Touring around, taking a bit of a break.' So that didn't help me much.

I picked a room that looked out over the field of cows. I don't think I realised how damp it was until it was time to go to bed. There was a distinctly musty smell in the air, and when I looked closely at the wallpaper I could see that in places it was coming away from the walls. My Mum and her sister are not a bit alike. I knew Mum would never let me sleep in a damp room. I wasn't sure what damp was supposed to do to you, but I knew it wasn't good.

When I got into bed, I didn't feel very sleepy. My aunt had given me a copy of the magazine she was working for, so I had a look at that. It was called *Holiday UK* and the cover 'London' printed across one corner and a colour picture of horses in a park. There was a great long article by my aunt inside, which went on for about six pages, with lots of photographs, and each one had her name up the side of it. But there were also adverts for hotels and restaurants and shops, along with a couple of pages listing places to eat, theatres, cinemas, that sort of stuff. Also it was free, so I realised it couldn't be up to much. Still, I knew they must somehow have enough money to pay her, or they couldn't send her rushing around the countryside like this.

Tip Strip

Question 1: Read the text carefully. What impresses the writer in the first paragraph? What turns out to be different when you read on?

Question 5: How much does the writer know about the purpose of the visit?

Question 8: What makes the writer think that the magazine is probably not very good?

1   What did the writer think of the farmhouse when she first saw it?

   A   It was better than the description in the guidebook.
   B   It lived up to her expectations of the countryside.
   C   It was similar to one her aunt had written about.
   D   It reminded her of her own house.

2   What does the word 'ridge' (line 7) describe?

   A   an agricultural building
   B   a feature of the landscape
   C   a piece of farm machinery
   D   a way of dividing fields on a farm

3   What do we discover about the farm in the second paragraph?

   A   It wasn't as large as it seemed.
   B   None of the animals belonged to it.
   C   The owner lived in another part of the country.
   D   The bed-and-breakfast business was doing well.

4   What disappointed the writer about the accommodation offered at the farm?

   A   the lack of space to hang clothes
   B   the fact that it needed cleaning
   C   the limited amount of furniture
   D   the size of the rooms

5   When Mrs Vosper asked if they were on holiday, the writer felt

   A   embarrassed by her aunt's reply.
   B   unsure why her aunt had really come.
   C   too tired to take in what was being said.
   D   worried that she might be asked something next.

6   What does the writer suggest about her bedroom at the farmhouse?

   A   Her aunt had picked a better one.
   B   It was an unhealthy place to sleep.
   C   Her mother would have approved of it.
   D   It wasn't the one she would have chosen.

7   The word 'it' in line 74 refers to

   A   a page in the magazine.
   B   an article in the magazine.
   C   a photograph in the magazine.
   D   an advertisement in the magazine.

8   The writer was unimpressed by the magazine because

   A   it didn't contain any interesting stories.
   B   it provided only factual information.
   C   it seemed to be all about London.
   D   it was given away free to people.

You are going to read an extract from an article about a trip to study the bottlenose whale. Seven sentences have been removed from the article. Choose from the sentences **A–H** the one which fits each gap (**9–15**). There is one extra sentence which you do not need to use.

Bottlenose whales, the deep divers of the North Atlantic

Douglas Chadwick joined the crew of the research boat the Balaena.

I have joined the crew of the *Balaena*, a 15-metre research boat, and we are now a few kilometres off the east coast of Canada, sailing over what seafarers call the *Gully*. Gully means 'narrow channel', but this it is more like a drowned Grand Canyon, about ten kilometres across and, in places, over a kilometre straight down to the bottom of the sea. The Gully, with its abundant fish, is home to a dozen kinds of cetaceans.

We have come in search of bottlenose whales. Hal Whitehead, a whale expert, and his crew are here to study the behaviour of these enigmatic creatures. I am hoping to see at least one today, but I am prepared to be disappointed. I've been told that, as a rule, the first things you see are spouts, the typical jets of water coming out of their heads, which are visible from a distance. **9**

The northern bottlenose and at least nineteen closely related middle-sized whales form the family *Ziphiidae*. Referred to as 'beaked whales', they account for one in every four species of cetaceans – the marine mammals known as whales, dolphins and porpoises. People love whales, but most of us wouldn't recognise a *ziphiid* if one surged through the living room. **10**

Already some three metres long at birth, northern bottlenoses continue to grow in size until the age of twenty, when they may reach ten metres. Adults weigh between five and seven tonnes, roughly the same as African elephants. **11** 'These are probably among the most intelligent animals on the entire planet, and we hardly know a thing about them,' says Hal Whitehead.

It is very quiet and all we can hear is the creak of the ship's masts as it sways. Suddenly, breaths like great sighs sound through the fog. **12** The smallest one swims for the boat and a larger companion cuts it off. Then they rejoin the others to float like swollen logs a short distance away.

I can see them well. They have small fins but big, domed heads with imposing foreheads above narrow, protruding jaws. Their heads are two-thirds out of the water now, all pointing our way. **13** We are being studied by northern bottlenose whales, which is only fair, since that is what we came to do to them.

If the bottlenoses don't swim too fast, we can keep up and observe them. Their movements are accompanied by grunts, whistles and cheers made by the blowholes. Every so often, one repeatedly lifts its tail to give the water a resounding slap. This display may function as yet another way to be heard. **14**

The biggest question is what goes on when these animals are not on the surface, which is most of the time. To find out, the researchers attached a time-depth recorder (TDR) to a whale's skin. The TDR stayed on for four-and-a-half hours and surfaced with the first solid data ever obtained about a *ziphiid* in its submarine kingdom. **15** This revelation seems to prove Hal Whitehead's theory that the world's deepest diver is the bottlenose whale – or maybe one of the many other beaked whales yet to be studied.

Tip Strip

Question 9: The sentence before the gap describes what you can see 'from a distance'. Find a sentence that refers to what happens when you get near.

Question 14: Before the gap there is a description of a display by the whales. Find a sentence that describes another display.

Question 15: Can you find a sentence that links 'the first solid data' and 'This revelation'?

A   This is not surprising because, even among scientists, these whales probably qualify as the least familiar of all big mammals.

B   On one of its dives, the bottlenose had reached a depth of 900 metres.

C   These animals aren't just watching us, they are scanning us with rapid clicking noises just above the range of human hearing.

D   Whale hunting reduced the population by at least seventy percent, and the species remains depleted today.

E   The same holds for leaping skyward and making a huge splash, though they may do this just for fun.

F   Beyond these basic facts, little is known about the lives of northern bottlenoses.

G   These strange noises come from four creatures, seven to ten metres long, which have risen from the depths.

H   When you come closer, though, you may find that they have submerged on a long dive, presumably in search of food.

You are going to read a magazine article about four women who are referees or umpires in different sports. For questions **16–30**, choose from the women (**A–D**). The women may be chosen more than once.

A	Bentla D'Couth
B	Ria Cortesio
C	Dr Gill Clarke
D	Grace Gavin

Which woman

mentions concentrating on her job and not paying attention to anything else? **16**

was appointed to do a job which she knew would be her last? **17**

remembers her feeling of confidence when she started refereeing? **18**

mentions one quality she has that is appreciated by male players? **19**

gives an example of the sort of tests she has had to go through? **20**

felt the need to prove to others that she was well suited to the job? **21**

says people feel more positive about her refereeing after seeing her in action? **22**

intends to do something so that other women can reach her position? **23**

feels that the general public is unaware of the demands of her job? **24**

remembers the excitement of learning about an appointment? **25**

mentions her good relations with other sports professionals? **26**

behaves differently when she's actually doing the job? **27**

refers to the lack of financial motivation in their work? **28**

admits one of her skills needs to be better to referee in men's matches? **29**

recognises an employer's positive attitude towards her sporting commitments? **30**

Bentla D'Couth   football referee

When you first meet Bentla D'Couth, the first woman football referee in India, appearances can be deceptive. She is soft-spoken and appears shy and unassuming, in sharp contrast to how she is on the field, where she appears loud and aggressive. Bentla was always interested in football, but it was only at the age of eighteen that she learnt that women's football existed. 'In my first refereeing job, I knew that I was very well aware of every detail of the game and that's why I could not go wrong. I was sure I wouldn't make a wrong decision,' she says. 'It doesn't happen now, but I guess earlier people did have that "what would she know" attitude. But once they saw me on the field refereeing a match, they would start coming to me for tips to improve their game. I can say that I haven't had any bad experiences so far.' Bentla knows she needs to improve on her positioning, though. 'Boys play very fast, so it can be a little taxing to keep up with their pace.'

Dr Gill Clarke   Olympics umpire

'Sydney was actually my third Olympics and this was a unique achievement as until then no British woman had ever umpired at three Games. It seemed a long time since my first Olympics in Barcelona in 1992, and then Atlanta in 1996.' A World and Olympic panel umpire's performance is assessed in all international matches, and they have to score a minimum 8 out of 10 every time if they want to maintain their position. 'Factors included in the assessment are such things as control, signals and cooperation with the other umpire on the pitch and fitness,' explains Clarke. She arrived in Sydney early to get over the stresses and strains of the flight, ready for the pressures of the two weeks of the Olympic hockey competition, knowing too that it would be her final tournament as she had decided to retire at what she hoped was the top. 'Increasingly, there is more at stake,' she says, 'it is big money for the players and the coaches but for umpires only personal satisfaction at a job well done.'

Ria Cortesio   baseball umpire

Ria Cortesio, a native of Davenport, Iowa, is one of five women to have umpired in professional baseball. She is hoping to open doors for others to follow her. Asked what drove her as a young person to become an umpire, she referred to 'the challenge'. 'I don't think that people realise what it means to work games day in and day out at the professional level, always on the road,' she said. 'It's you against the world during the season.' Asked about her interactions with fans during the game last Sunday, she said she was so focussed on her work that she didn't have time to consider her surroundings. 'It really doesn't make any difference being a woman on the field – or even off the field. I do feel a great responsibility to get girls and women involved. The one group of people that I haven't had a single problem with are the players, coaches or managers. If anything, there are some that are more respectful to me than usual.'

Grace Gavin   rugby referee

When Grace Gavin was accepted as a referee for the Women's Rugby World Cup, she found out via her mobile phone on her way to the airport. 'I almost bounced myself out of the taxi,' she says. Grace combines her refereeing with a full-time job. 'I strongly believe that if we referee world-class athletes, we must train like world-class athletes. This is difficult to manage when work occupies fifty to sixty hours of my week. My firm is very supportive, though. Of course, my boss was happy when I retired from playing because the black eyes that I sported some Monday mornings were not going down well with clients.' Early in her refereeing career, somebody told her that she would always be handicapped by the perception that she was not fast enough to referee men's rugby. 'I have worked constantly to defeat this perception,' she says. 'Surprisingly, many players like having me as a ref because they can hear my voice. They can pick it out and are able to respond in the heat of the match.'

You **must** answer this question. Write your answer in **120–150** words in an appropriate style.

1   You recently won a prize in a sports competition. The prize is a free week at a seaside resort of your choice. You have just received this letter from the competition organiser. Read the letter and the notes you have made. Then write a letter to the organiser, using **all** your notes.

I am very pleased to send you some information about your prize – a free week at a holiday resort of your choice, for two people.

Your prize includes the following:

provide more details? —

which? —

- free return tickets — *by plane or coach?*
- accommodation
- meals — *all?*
- tickets for sports performances

Not included: travel insurance

I now need to know which holiday resort you would like to go to, when you would like to travel and the name and age of the person travelling with you.

I look forward to hearing from you.

Yours sincerely,

Paula Holden

Competition Organiser

Write your **letter**. You must use grammatically correct sentences with accurate spelling and punctuation in a style appropriate for the situation.

Tip Strip
Question 1
Have you included these points?
1 the kind of transport
2 what other information you need, e.g. what hotel
3 whether breakfast, lunch and dinner are provided
4 mentioned sports you like

Tip Strip

Question 2

Have you included these points?

1 what inexpensive/free music events are available

2 visits to museums, giving reasons for your choices

3 how you can plan the week to make the most of the time.

Question 3

Have you included these points?

1 whether you liked the songs and why

2 something about the musicians (clothes, friendliness, quality, etc)

3 whether the school was a good venue: large enough, acoustics, facilities, etc

Question 4

• Describe what happened. Remember it must be frightening (who or what frightened Sarah?).

• Explain how the problem is resolved. Remember it must end well for Sarah.

Question 5(a)

• Include details about why the character is not pleasant (e.g. appearance, behaviour, feelings, rudeness, etc). Choose at least two characters who were affected by it and give specific examples.

Question 5(b)

• Write about the aspects of the book which you think make it suitable or unsuitable for teenagers. Remember to give reasons for your opinions by referring to the plot, the characters, etc.

Write an answer to **one** of the questions 2–4 in this part. Write an answer in **120–180** words in an appropriate style.

---

2   Your English friend is coming to visit you next month and this is part of an email he has sent you.

> *I am really looking forward to this trip, but you know me, I like to plan everything well! I would very much like to go and see as much music as possible, without spending too much money, and also visit a few museums. Have you had any thoughts about how we could make the most of the week?*
>
> *Simon*

Write your **email**.

3   You recently saw this notice in the college newsletter.

> **Write a review of the school concert!**
>
> What did you think of the school concert? Write a review for the school magazine. Include your opinion about the choice of songs, the performers and say whether you think the school hall is a suitable venue.
>
> The best review will be published!

Write your **review**.

4   Your teacher has asked you to write a story for an international magazine. The story must **end** with the following words:

It had all ended well, but Sarah would never be able to forget how frightened she had been.

Write your **story**.

5   Answer **one** of the following two questions based on your reading of **one** of these set books.

(a) Author – *Name of book*
There is one character in the book who is not very pleasant. Write an **essay** describing this character and explaining how his/her behaviour affected other characters in the novel.

(b) Author – *Name of book*
Would you recommend this book to teenagers all over the world? Write a **review** for the library magazine saying in what ways the book is or isn't suitable and give reasons for your opinions.

Part 1

For questions **1–12**, read the text below and decide which answer (**A**, **B**, **C** or **D**) best fits each gap. There is an example at the beginning **(0)**.

In the exam you mark your answers on a separate answer sheet

Example:

0 **A** goes **B** calls **C** passes **D** titles

Sudoku

Tip Strip

Question 4: Which of these words can be followed by the preposition 'for'?

Question 7: Which word normally collocates with 'work'?

Question 11: Only one of these words is correct in the context of the Internet.

Question 12: Which of these words will make a phrasal verb which means 'had the idea'?

Are you a fan of the popular logical puzzle that **(0)** ...... by the name Sudoku? **(1)** ...... you're not, the chances are you know somebody who is. Once **(2)** ...... known outside Japan, this addictive brain teaser has become a common feature of newspaper puzzle pages all over the world.

Sudoku's great success **(3)** ...... much to its simplicity. The game **(4)** ...... for neither mathematical ability nor **(5)** ...... knowledge and there are just a few sentences of straightforward instructions to read before you can play. The only skill required is the ability to **(6)** ...... the difference between nine different symbols, and these don't even have to be numbers.

Some clever marketing has helped the game. Western newspapers worked **(7)** ...... at promoting the game. Without this, it is unlikely that it would have **(8)** ...... off and become quite such a runaway success. The game also **(9)** ...... from its Japanese name that made people in many parts of the world **(10)** ...... it as a superior kind of puzzle compared to those you usually find in newspapers and magazines.

But the popularity of Sudoku reached a peak in 2006, if the number of **(11)** ...... on one leading website is anything to go by. Newspapers responded by **(12)** ...... up with new kinds of logical puzzles, all with simple rules and Japanese names. But for true Sudoku fans, only the real thing will do.

0	**A** goes	**B** calls	**C** passes	**D** titles
1	**A** Apart from	**B** Even if	**C** In spite of	**D** Regardless
2	**A** thinly	**B** rarely	**C** hardly	**D** briefly
3	**A** results	**B** thanks	**C** owes	**D** lends
4	**A** expects	**B** demands	**C** requests	**D** calls
5	**A** general	**B** normal	**C** usual	**D** ordinary
6	**A** copy	**B** match	**C** notice	**D** recognise
7	**A** tough	**B** hard	**C** strong	**D** heavy
8	**A** got	**B** taken	**C** given	**D** passed
9	**A** promoted	**B** improved	**C** benefited	**D** increased
10	**A** believe	**B** regard	**C** think	**D** consider
11	**A** hits	**B** clicks	**C** strikes	**D** shots
12	**A** setting	**B** putting	**C** making	**D** coming

For questions **13–24**, read the text below and think of the word which best fits each gap. Use only **one** word in each gap. There is an example at the beginning (**0**).

In the exam you write your answers IN CAPITAL LETTERS on a separate answer sheet.

Example: | 0 | W | E | R | E | | | | | | |

The birth of *YouTube*

Tip Strip

Question 16: This verb combines with 'up' after the pronoun to make a phrasal verb.

Question 19: Which word will complete the comparative expression?

Question 20: Which preposition will complete the common expression?

Question 22: Which preposition is used before 'average'?

In 2005, Chad Hurley and Steve Chen, two software designers from Silicon Valley in California, (**0**) ...... invited to a dinner party. Several people had brought their camcorders to the party and these people were complaining about (**13**) ...... difficult it was to share home videos online. That was when Chad and Steve came up (**14**) ...... the idea for *YouTube*, the site which makes (**15**) ...... easy to upload home videos onto the Internet. They formed a company, borrowed some money and (**16**) ...... themselves up in business.

It turned (**17**) ...... that millions of people already had short home video clips that they thought it (**18**) ...... be fun to share with other enthusiasts around the world. Launched in December 2005, *YouTube* soon contained more (**19**) ...... a million short video clips. People were uploading 8000 clips a day, and watching three million a day. They had mostly heard about the site through word (**20**) ...... mouth, email and hyperlink, and eighty percent of the clips had (**21**) ...... made by amateurs.

So why was *YouTube* such an immediate success? Researchers found that, (**22**) ...... average, people were spending fifteen minutes on the site during each visit, (**23**) ...... was enough time to view several short funny clips. In (**24**) ...... words, they were using *YouTube* to give them a little break from their work or study.

Part 3

For questions **25–34**, read the text below. Use the word given in capitals at the end of some of the lines to form a word that fits the gap **in the same line**. There is an example at the beginning **(0)**.

In the exam you write your answers IN CAPITAL LETTERS on a separate answer sheet.

Example:

| 0 | I | N | C | R | E | A | S | I | N | G | |

Putting the fun back into driving

Tip Strip

Question 25: Is a noun or an adjective needed here?

Question 26: Add a suffix to this adjective to make the noun.

Question 30: What's the word for people who drive cars?

Question 34: How does the end of this verb change when it becomes a noun?

Because of the **(0)** ...... number of cars on the roads, few   **INCREASE**

people get the chance to go out driving for **(25)** ...... these days.   **PLEASE**

In Britain, traffic **(26)** ...... has increased by over seventy percent in   **DENSE**

the last couple of decades, but there has been relatively little **(27)** ......   **GROW**

in the country's road network. The result of more traffic on the roads

has been a greater emphasis on road **(28)** ...... and this has meant   **SAFE**

the **(29)** ...... of tougher speed regulations. As a result, those   **INTRODUCE**

(30) ...... who enjoy going fast are always in danger of being fined.   **MOTOR**

One answer is something called a 'track day'. This is an event where

people can drive their own cars around a racing circuit, and explore

the limits of its **(31)** ...... without the need to worry about other   **PERFORM**

road users. Track days are not competitive events, and people go

for the pure **(32)** ...... of driving. Track days are currently seeing   **ENJOY**

an enormous boom in **(33)** ...... , with over six hundred a year   **POPULAR**

held in Britain alone. A great **(34)** ...... of vehicles can be found   **VARY**

on the track at the same time and drivers have to follow a few

basic rules. For example, slower vehicles must allow faster ones to

pass.

Part 4

For questions **35–42**, complete the second sentence so that it has a similar meaning to the first sentence, using the word given. **Do not change the word given.** You must use between **two** and **five** words, including the word given. Here is an example **(0)**.

Example:

0   What type of music do you like best?

FAVOURITE

What .... type of music?

The gap can be filled by the words 'is your favourite', so you write:

Example: | 0 | | IS YOUR FAVOURITE |

In the exam you write only the missing words IN CAPITAL LETTERS on a separate answer sheet.

Tip Strip

Question 35: You need to form a comparative expression using 'as'.

Question 36: What comes after this verb in reported speech – a gerund or an infinitive?

Question 39: Which multi-verb word means 'to participate'?

Question 41: What's the past participle of the verb 'to choose'?

35   I expected ice-skating to be more difficult than it actually was.

NOT

Ice-skating .... as I had expected.

36   'Leon, I think you should tell your mother the truth,' said Maite.

ADVISED

Maite .... his mother the truth.

37   Not many people went to see that live concert in the park.

NUMBER

Only .... went to see that live concert in the park.

38   Naomi hasn't seen any of her cousins for years.

SAW

It's .... any of her cousins.

39 How many competitors went in for the race?

PART

How many competitors .... the race?

40 You can borrow my new bicycle, but you must be careful with it.

LONG

You can borrow my new bicycle .... careful with it.

41 Melanie regretted choosing such an expensive jacket.

WISHED

Melanie .... a less expensive jacket.

42 Recycling old newspapers seems pointless to me.

POINT

I can't .... old newspapers.

Part 1

You will hear people talking in eight different situations. For questions **1–8**, choose the best answer (**A**, **B** or **C**).

Tip Strip

Question 3: Does the speaker say you should pay attention to the scales or to your diet?

Question 4: The man mentions three points, but the woman agrees with only one of them. Which one is it?

Question 6: What is the purpose of the speaker, to say what the sport is like, to inform us of its possible dangers, or to say we should try it?

1   You hear a man talking about a ceramics course he attended.

What aspect of the course did he find unsatisfactory?

A   the level of support from the staff

B   the quality of the materials

C   the cost for students

| | 1 |

2   On a radio programme, you hear some information about a future guest.

What will he be talking about?

A   organising a mountain holiday

B   learning mountain-climbing skills

C   buying mountaineering equipment

| | 2 |

3   You hear part of a talk about how to look fit and healthy.

What is the speaker's advice?

A   check your weight regularly

B   build up your muscles

C   avoid certain foods

| | 3 |

4   You overhear two college students talking about applying for a weekend job.

What do they agree about?

A   It would be an enjoyable thing to do.

B   It would be useful experience for the future.

C   It would help them with their college expenses.

| | 4 |

5 You overhear two people talking about transport.

Why has the woman decided to use a bike instead of a car?

A She hopes the exercise will improve her health.

B She is concerned about the environment.

C She can no longer afford the cost.

	5

6 On the radio, you hear a woman talking about a sport.

What is she doing?

A explaining something to us

B warning us about something

C recommending something to us

	6

7 You hear the weather forecast on the radio.

How will the weather change tomorrow?

A It will get colder.

B It will get sunnier.

C It will get windier.

	7

8 You hear a radio presenter talking about a theatre.

What does he say about it?

A It is offering an impressive programme.

B It will be closed down in the near future.

C It has received a grant for improvements.

	8

You will hear a talk on the radio about the Loch Ness Monster. For questions **9–18**, complete the sentences.

The mysterious monster

The head of the Loch Ness Monster has been compared to that of a

[**9**]

The first published photographic image of the monster is known as the

[**10**] picture.

People argued that a picture taken in 1960 actually showed a

[**11**], but experts have proved them wrong.

Tim Dinsdale realised that most monster sightings occurred on days when the

weather was [**12**]

Most eyewitnesses say they have no interest in getting

[**13**] when they report their sightings.

In 1968, an underwater investigation used sonar equipment instead of

[**14**] to try and find the monster.

An attempt to find the monster by using a [**15**]

failed in 1969 because the Loch Ness water is so dirty.

The idea of using a group of [**16**] to help with

the search proved to be too complicated.

Dr Rines' underwater picture of 1972 seemed to show the

[**17**] of a large sea animal.

The aim of the latest research project is to study all the

[*and* **18**] living in Loch Ness.

Part 3

You will hear five different people talking about concerts they went to. For questions **19–23**, choose from the list (**A–F**) the opinion each speaker expresses about the concert. Use the letters only once. There is one extra letter which you do not need to use.

Tip Strip

B: Listen for a speaker who compares the musicians' live performances to the CDs they record in a studio.

C: Speakers 1 and 2 criticise the performers, but who mentions an improvement?

F: Speakers 1 and 3 mention good causes, but who is referring to this particular concert?

A The performers got a better reception than they deserved.

Speaker 1 ☐ **19**

B These musicians are at their best in live performances.

Speaker 2 ☐ **20**

C The concert improved after a disappointing beginning.

Speaker 3 ☐ **21**

D I enjoyed the band's choice of material for the concert.

Speaker 4 ☐ **22**

E I'd like to have seen more bands for the price I paid.

Speaker 5 ☐ **23**

F I was pleased the concert was raising money for a good cause.

Part 4

You will hear an interview with Patrick Shaw, who works as a pilot for a company that organises hot-air balloon trips. For questions **24–30**, choose the best answer (**A**, **B** or **C**).

Tip Strip

Question 25: Do members of the ground crew get paid for their work? Do they get a chance to fly while they are doing their job?

Question 26: Read the first line carefully and underline 'particularly difficult'. The speaker mentions a few difficulties, but which one is the most serious?

Question 28: Read the first line carefully and underline the word 'unsatisfactory'. You are listening for something that Patrick does not like.

24 According to Patrick, what worries people most when they take a balloon trip?

   A how far the wind will take them
   B whether they will hit some obstacle
   C what the experience of landing will be like

24

25 Why does Patrick recommend joining the ground crew?

   A It's the best way of learning about balloons.
   B It provides some experience of flying a balloon.
   C It can be a fun way of earning extra income.

25

26 What makes the job of the ground crew particularly difficult?

   A poor communication with the pilot
   B unpredictable weather conditions
   C the nervousness of the passengers

26

27 Patrick says that all members of the ground crew must

   A be physically strong.
   B have good social skills.
   C know their area well.

27

28 Patrick finds it unsatisfactory when new crew members

   A fail to cooperate with each other.
   B distract him with unnecessary questions.
   C don't accept the way things should be done.

28

29 What does Patrick say about balloon competitions?

   A It is often difficult to determine who has won.
   B The finishing target area is often unmarked.
   C Some competitors are requesting clearer rules.

29

30 Patrick thinks his particular skills as a pilot result from

   A the way in which he was trained.
   B the fact that he's adventurous by nature.
   C the amount of experience he has.

30

Part 1 (3 minutes)

Answer these questions:

Do you have any brothers and sisters?

Tell us something about the place where you are living at the moment.

What do the other members of your family do?

Part 2 (3 or 4 minutes)

Holiday destinations (compare, contrast and speculate)

Turn to pictures 1 and 2 on page 127, which show people enjoying their holidays.

Candidate A, compare and contrast these photographs, and say what type of person would choose these holidays. You have a minute to do this.

Candidate B, do you like beach holidays?

Waiting (compare, contrast and speculate)

Turn to pictures 1 and 2 on page 128, which show people waiting.

Candidate B, compare and contrast these photographs, and say how the people may be feeling. You have a minute to do this.

Candidate A, do you mind having to wait sometimes?

Part 3 (3 or 4 minutes)

Jobs at open-air concerts (discuss and evaluate)

Turn to the pictures on page 129, which show jobs at an open-air concert. Imagine a college is organising a series of concerts by local bands and they have asked students to help.

How difficult or easy might it be to do these jobs?

What skills are needed to do them well?

Which would be the most popular with the students?

Part 4 (3 or 4 minutes)

Answer these questions:

Have you ever been to an open-air concert? What was it like?

What's your favourite band? Have you seen it/them live?

What instrument would you most like to be able to play well?

TEST 3: READING

Part 1

You are going to read a magazine article about a language course. For questions 1–8, choose the answer (A, B, C or D) which you think fits best according to the text.

Travelling to learn

Having decided in later life that it might actually be quite nice to master another language, rather than dusting off my schoolgirl French, I opted for a clean break: Spanish. Three years of half-finished evening classes later, thanks to the enthusiastic teacher's efforts I could order in a restaurant and ask directions, but my conversational skills were limited to asking everybody how many brothers and sisters they had. The only true way to master a language is to live and breathe it for a period of time. I toyed with the idea of taking a language 'immersion' course abroad, but two little words always stopped me: home stay. Then I saw that tour operator *Journey Latin America* had started offering Spanish courses in Peru, amongst other places. The opportunity to realise two long-held ambitions in one holiday – to improve my Spanish and to see Machu Picchu – proved irresistible.

21   My misgivings evaporate the moment I am met by my home-stay family, the Rojas, at Cusco airport. They greet me warmly, like an old friend. Carlos is an optician and Carmucha owns a restaurant. With their four children they live in a comfortable house right in the centre of town. Then I'm whisked off to a family friend's birthday party, where I understand nothing apart from the bit where they sing 'Happy Birthday'. By the end of the evening my face aches from holding an expression of polite, but uncomprehending interest, and I fall into bed wondering what I've let myself in for.

The following morning, I'm off to school and get to know my new school chums. We're aged between 19 and 65, each spending up to a month studying before travelling around Peru. We had all clearly hit it off with our new families, though one of us is a bit alarmed at the blue flame that jumps out of the shower switch in the morning, one of us has a long bus ride in to the school, and another is disconcerted to find that his host mother is actually six years younger than he is. We're all keen to meet our teachers and see which class we'll be joining, but after sitting the placement test, we learn that as it's not yet high season and the school is not too busy, tuition will be one-on-one. Although

49   some find the prospect daunting, to my mind, this is a pretty impressive ratio – though even in high season the maximum class size swells to only four pupils.

As the week unfolds, I slip into a routine. Four hours of classes in the morning, back home for lunch, then afternoons free for sightseeing. Cusco will supply anything it can

57   to lure the feckless student away from his or her homework. It's all too easy to swap verb conjugations for a swift beer in a bar, although it's at least three days before anybody plucks up the courage to suggest that maybe we don't have to go back to our respective families for dinner every night. Once the seed of rebellion has been planted we queue up like nervous teenagers outside the phone box plucking up the courage to ring our 'Mums' and ask if we can stay out late – all the more strange when you consider that our average age is probably thirty-three. But after one strangely unsatisfying restaurant meal, I decide that true authenticity is back home at the dinner table with Carmucha.

As the week wears on, a strange thing starts to happen: the dinner-table chatter, which at first was so much 'white noise', starts to have some meaning and, miraculously, I can follow the thread of the conversation. What's more, I've started to dream in Spanish!

Tip Strip

Question 1: The teacher succeeded in teaching her to do simple things, but why is the writer unhappy?

Question 5: What complaints do some of her classmates have?

Question 7: Read the next line carefully for a description of what a 'feckless' student would do.

1   How did the writer feel after her courses of evening classes?

   A   proud of what she'd learnt so far
   B   frustrated at her slow rate of progress
   C   critical of the attitude adopted by her teacher
   D   unable to perform simple tasks in the language

2   What put the writer off the idea of doing an 'immersion' course?

   A   having relatively little time to devote to it
   B   the thought of staying with a host family
   C   her own lack of fluency in the language
   D   the limited range of locations available

3   The word 'misgivings' (line 21) refers to the writer's

   A   reasons for choosing Peru for her trip.
   B   first impressions of the city of Cusco.
   C   plans to do more than learn the language.
   D   doubts about her decision to come on the trip.

4   How did the writer feel after the party she attended?

   A   upset that people assumed she could speak Spanish
   B   confident that she was beginning to make progress
   C   unsure how well she would cope during her stay
   D   worried that she may have seemed rude

5   What did the writer discover when she met her fellow students?

   A   Some were less happy with the arrangements than she was.
   B   They would all be studying together for a fixed period.
   C   Some were much older than the teachers at the school.
   D   They did not all like their host families.

6   The word 'daunting' (line 49) suggests that the writer's fellow students viewed one-to-one lessons as

   A   a disappointing change of plan.
   B   good value for money.
   C   an unexpected bonus.
   D   a difficult challenge.

7   A 'feckless' student (line 57) is one who

   A   plans study time carefully.
   B   is easily distracted from studying.
   C   completes all homework efficiently.
   D   balances study with other activities.

8   How did the writer feel when her fellow students suggested a night out together?

   A   embarrassed by their immaturity
   B   thinks her hosts are too rebellious
   C   amused by their behaviour
   D   unwilling to take part

You are going to read an article about the use of robots. Seven sentences have been removed from the article. Choose from the sentences **A–H** the one which fits each gap (**9–15**). There is one extra sentence which you do not need to use.

If you're happy, the robot knows it

Robots are gaining the ability to engage us emotionally, giving them a much broader range of uses.

RoCo, the world's first expressive computer, has a monitor for a head and a simple LCD screen for a face. Inhabiting a back room in the Massachusetts Institute of Technology's media lab, RoCo has a double-jointed neck which allows it to shift the monitor up and down, tilt it forward and back, and move it from side to side. **9** When you hang your head and sink into your chair, RoCo tilts forward and drops low to almost touch the desk, mimicking your gloomy posture. When you perk up and straighten your back, it spots the change and cheerfully swings forward and upward.

RoCo was unveiled at a human-robot interaction conference in Washington DC in March 2007. Because it responds to a user's changes in posture, its creators hope people might be more likely to build up a relationship with the computer that will make sitting at a desk all day a little more enjoyable. **10**

The team is among a growing number of researchers who are investigating how far a robot's physical presence can influence people. **11** Researchers at Stanford University in California have already proved that an in-car assistance system, for example, can make us drive more carefully if the voice matches our mood. But robots can have a greater impact. 'If it can actually touch you, it's a lot more meaningful,'

says Cynthia Breazeal of the Media Lab, who created RoCo with her colleague Rosalind Picard.

Breazeal suggests that RoCo could be programmed to adopt the right posture to foster greater attention and persistence in children. **12** To find out, Aaron Powers at iRobot in Burlington, Massachusetts, and colleagues at Carnegie Mellon University in Pittsburgh, Pennsylvania, invited volunteers to chat about health and happiness with a 1.3-metre-tall, talking humanoid robot called Pearl. They then compared their impressions with those of people who had only heard the robot and seen its projected image.

They found that volunteers rated the physical robot as more trustworthy, sociable, responsive, competent, respectful and lifelike than the projected image of the robot. More importantly, the researchers also found that the physical robot had the most influence over the volunteers. **13**

This persuasive power is important and is already being put to use in the classroom. Hiroshi Ishiguro, a roboticist at Osaka University in Japan, has developed a remote-controlled robotic clone of himself called Germinoid-H1. **14** Interestingly, his students preferred this to a video or telephone link.

The emphasis is now on the improvement of teamwork and task coordination between humans and robots. But the idea of robots as team-mates is not universally accepted. **15** Breazeal argues that this can be resolved by training people and robots together, so that we learn the robot's limitations in advance. 'There might be initial disappointment, but five minutes later we will have figured it out,' she says.

Tip Strip

Question 9: The sentences after the gap describe the movements of the robot and of the user. Find a sentence that refers to them.

Question 12: The sentence after the gap begins with 'To find out'. Find out what?

Question 13: Find a sentence that proves that the physical robot 'had the most influence'.

A But does a physical robot really provoke a greater response in people than a much cheaper animated agent on a computer screen could?

B An attached camera can detect when the user changes position, allowing RoCo to adjust its posture accordingly.

C This does not mean that the robots of the future may be able to see things from our point of view and correct us when we make bad decisions.

D Using technology to manipulate someone or shape their mood is nothing new.

E Because robots have no drive to protect themselves, they cannot protect the group, says Victoria Groom, a researcher in human-robot interaction.

F The robot had actually prompted lots of participants to declare that they would take up more healthy activities, such as exercising and avoiding fatty foods.

G They also believe that by tuning into users' moods, the robot might help them to get their work done more effectively.

H Recently he has begun using it to represent him at meetings and classes at the Advanced Telecommunications Research Institute when he can't attend in person.

You are going to read a magazine article about wild camping. For questions **16–30**, choose from the people (**A–D**). The people may be chosen more than once.

A	**Luis Gallivan**
B	**Anna Cresswell**
C	**Thomas Parsons**
D	**Jennie Martinez**

Which person

enjoys the idea of facing some risks while camping? **16**

compares attitudes to wild camping now and in the past? **17**

mentions the inexpensive nature of wild camping? **18** **19**

was forced by circumstances to share a camping experience? **20**

is unwilling to recommend areas suitable for wild camping? **21**

is pleased to have shown others how to enjoy camping? **22**

accepts that parents may be concerned about their children? **23**

refers to the need to travel light when wild camping? **24**

explains how a negative experience made her avoid camping for a while? **25**

says more people are beginning to see the attraction of wild camping? **26**

describes a dangerous situation which could have been avoided? **27**

says inexperienced campers should not go to remote places? **28**

gives reasons for disliking organised campsites? **29**

mentions being unable to do without certain comforts? **30**

Luis Gallivan I'm turning my back on organised sites, particularly the supersized ones. Even at the relatively quiet sites you can seldom escape the constant chattering of people in neighbouring tents, or worse still, the noise of satellite-assisted televisions from camper vans. I go wild camping, which means I can set up my tent in a field or on a mountainside without paying anyone for the privilege. Lots of 'mild campers' (that's what we call the ones who use campsites) are waking up to the fact that wild camping gives you an eco-friendly break and offers a great deal more in the way of adventure. Because it's so different from 'mild' camping, though, people need to ask themselves: 'Do I really need this?' before packing their stuff. Wild camping is the ultimate budget holiday – once you've got to wherever you're going, the only expense is feeding yourself.

Anna Cresswell My first experience of wild camping was a bit of an accident. I'd trekked with a friend to a remote spot but we each had different plans. She wanted to stay the night in a tent, whilst I was wanted to head back home before bedtime. As it happened, I was so exhausted that I ended up sharing the tiny uncomfortable tent with her. I must say the experience put me off wild camping for months, until I reminded myself that if I hadn't stayed, I'd never have witnessed that breathtaking sunset which more than made up for all the discomfort. Then there's the excitement that comes from making yourself slightly vulnerable: out in the wild with nobody watching over you. And I never have to book, if the weather's disappointing I don't go, if it turns cold I go home. This is as stress-free as holidays get. But I'm a bit fussy about taking everything I need, even if it means a heavier backpack: for example, I must have a folding chair, a thin self-inflating mattress and a pile of good books.

Wild camping

Camping in the wild rather than at organised campsites is a great way of getting away from it all and getting back to nature. Four experienced wild campers tell us why.

Thomas Parsons Perhaps the main reason why many people shy away from wild camping is our modern-day culture of 'risk aversion' – in other words, avoiding all activities that seem in any way dangerous, however unlikely it is that anything would actually go wrong. In less paranoid times, wild camping was indeed very common, but people nowadays want safe environments, especially when it comes to feeling at ease with what their kids are doing, and organised campsites are the obvious answer. I'm not keen to suggest good places to go wild camping, though, because one of the joys of the activity comes from finding places nobody else knows about. For the beginner, I'd advise places which aren't too far from civilisation in case anything does go wrong. I learnt the hard way, weighing myself down with unnecessary home comforts and camping gadgets when apart from the usual backpacker's tent, warm sleeping bag, spare clothes and food, all you really need is a torch, lightweight cooking equipment, a map and a compass.

Jennie Martinez Camping was an integral part of my early years, and I've managed to pass on some of my enthusiasm to my own children. In striving for little luxuries like hot showers, 'mild' campers miss out on the delights of wild camping. There are very comfortable state-of-the-art tents available nowadays if you want a bit of comfort, and they don't cost that much. Once you're hooked on wild camping, nothing else will do and you get not to mind occasional problems with ants or wasps. The lack of fellow travellers makes me feel that the great views and the starlit skies have been laid on expressly for my own personal enjoyment. But camping in wild places also means having to observe a few basic rules. For instance, during a particularly dry season, it's best to avoid high fire-risk areas. I'll always remember a time when I was camping with friends and we noticed that somebody had failed to extinguish a small fire completely. We managed to put it out, but it could have been a disaster.

You **must** answer this question. Write your answer in **120–150** words in an appropriate style.

1   You want to improve your conversation skills in English. You have seen this advertisement in a newspaper, but you want more information. Read the advertisement and the notes you have made. Then write a letter to the school secretary, using **all** your notes.

GREEN HILL INSTITUTE
Green Hill Street
London
SW3

DO YOU WANT TO IMPROVE YOUR ENGLISH CONVERSATION SKILLS THIS SUMMER?

WE HAVE CLASSES FOR ALL LEVELS IN SMALL GROUPS!

REGISTER FOR AN INTENSIVE COURSE FOR FAST PROGRESS

PRICES FROM £150 A WEEK

SOCIAL AND CULTURAL ACTIVITIES INCLUDED IN THE PRICE

WE CAN ARRANGE YOUR ACCOMMODATION IN A GUEST HOUSE OR WITH A FAMILY

WRITE FOR A BROCHURE AND MORE INFORMATION TO:

ANDREW SIMMS
SECRETARY

How many at advanced level?

not clear how often

What are these?

prefer family, but price?

Write your **letter**. You must use grammatically correct sentences with accurate spelling and punctuation in a style appropriate for the situation.

Tip Strip

Question 1

Have you included these points?

1 Ask about number of students at advanced level.

2 Ask how many hours/ classes there are in intensive courses.

3 Say you would like to know what these activities are.

4 Explain you would prefer a family if it is not expensive.

Tip Strip

Question 2

Have you included these points?

1 A description of your favourite sport (why you enjoy it, what equipment you use, etc).

2 How old you were when you started, why you started, who you played with, etc.

3 Explain how it would help make friends.

Question 3

Remember the main purpose of a review is to give a personal opinion. You must give the reader a clear impression of the quality of what you are reviewing.

Have you included these points?

1 what the comedy show is about

2 what parts made you laugh most and why

3 whether the comedians were good actors, and why you think so

4 reasons for recommending it (or not) to other students

Question 4

Say what the summer job is, how much or how little you like it, whether you find it difficult to work when other people are on holiday. Mention any free time you get and how much you earn.

Question 5(a)

You can agree or disagree completely, or you can agree to a certain extent. If you argue that the plot is difficult to follow, explain why and give examples, e.g. not clear what is happening, too many characters make it confusing, narrative is sometimes in the past and sometimes in the present.

Question 5(b)

Choose a character who made an impression on you, describe him/her and say why. Refer to his/her personality, looks, behaviour, influence on other characters, etc.

Write an answer to **one** of the questions **2–4** in this part. Write an answer in **120–180** words in an appropriate style.

---

2 You have seen an announcement in an English language magazine called *Leisure Time*.

> ### My favourite sport
>
> Tell us about your favourite sport, when you started playing it, and if you would recommend it to young people who want to make new friends.
>
> The best article will get a surprise gift.

Write your **article**.

3 You recently saw this notice in the local newspaper.

> ### Have you seen a comedy show recently?
>
> Write a review for our paper and you may win free tickets for all Saturday shows! Say what parts were particularly funny, what you thought of the comedians and whether you would recommend it to other students.

Write your **review**.

4 This is part of an email you have received from a friend.

When you wrote last you said you had just started a summer job. How is it going? Is it hard to be working in the summer? Do you get any free time? Are the wages good?

Write your **email**.

5 Answer **one** of the following two questions based on your reading of **one** of these set books.

(a) Author – *Name of book*
Some critics have said that the plot of this book is difficult to follow. Write an **essay** saying whether you agree or disagree with this criticism, giving examples from the book to back up your opinions.

(b) Author – *Name of book*

I have read the book you recommended and I would like to know which character made the greatest impression on you. I'll tell you later about my own choice! Jon

Write a **letter** to Jon answering his question and explaining why the character made such an impression on you.

Part 1

For questions **1–12**, read the text below and decide which answer (**A**, **B**, **C** or **D**) best fits each gap. There is an example at the beginning (**0**).

In the exam you mark your answers on a separate answer sheet.

Example:

0 A founded   **B** invented   **C** originated   **D** discovered

0	A	B	C	D
	▬	▭	▭	▭

Boots for Africa

Tip Strip

Question 1: Which verb will combine with 'forces' to form a multi-word verb meaning 'cooperate with'?

Question 4: Which of the words is usually followed by the preposition 'in'?

Question 11: Which of the words collocates with 'a donation'?

Sheffield Football Club was (**0**) ...... one-hundred-and-fifty years ago, and is the oldest in the world. As part of its anniversary celebrations, the club has (**1**) ...... forces with the world's largest express transportation company, *FedEx Express*, in a charitable scheme (**2**) ...... as *Boots for Africa*. The (**3**) ...... of the scheme is to send more than two thousand pairs of used football boots to South Africa. The boots will be given to young people living in remote rural areas who are (**4**) ...... in taking up the sport and (**5**) ...... up local teams.

Sports organisations in Africa are giving their (**6**) ...... support to the scheme which will help make the game more accessible to thousands of young people and could have a beneficial (**7**) ...... on the country's performance in future World Cup championships.

People in Sheffield are, (**8**) ...... , being asked to donate any football boots, astro boots or football trainers of any size to the scheme. All the boots donated must be in good (**9**) ...... , complete with laces and studs. Local businesses and schools who may be able to donate more than one pair of boots can receive a special 'group donation pack'. This pack (**10**) ...... posters and leaflets, which can be used to publicise the scheme, plus collection bags to encourage people to (**11**) ...... a donation. The club's website has (**12**) ...... information about the scheme.

0	**A**	founded	**B**	invented	**C**	originated	**D**	discovered
1	**A**	tied	**B**	added	**C**	joined	**D**	linked
2	**A**	named	**B**	known	**C**	called	**D**	titled
3	**A**	ambition	**B**	motive	**C**	reason	**D**	aim
4	**A**	interested	**B**	curious	**C**	keen	**D**	attracted
5	**A**	coming	**B**	setting	**C**	beginning	**D**	finding
6	**A**	whole	**B**	full	**C**	entire	**D**	thorough
7	**A**	conclusion	**B**	result	**C**	effect	**D**	reaction
8	**A**	despite	**B**	however	**C**	although	**D**	therefore
9	**A**	fitness	**B**	state	**C**	condition	**D**	form
10	**A**	contains	**B**	complies	**C**	composes	**D**	consists
11	**A**	put	**B**	do	**C**	hand	**D**	make
12	**A**	greater	**B**	further	**C**	wider	**D**	larger

For questions **13–24**, read the text below and think of the word which best fits each gap. Use only **one** word in each gap. There is an example at the beginning **(0)**.

In the exam you write your answers IN CAPITAL LETTERS on a separate answer sheet.

Example: | 0 | M | O | S | T | | | | | | |

An influential cook

Delia Smith is one of the **(0)** ...... widely respected cookery writers in Britain. She has made regular appearances in television cookery programmes **(13)** ...... over thirty years, and more than ten million copies of her cookery books have **(14)** ...... sold.

Delia always says that her real skill is communication **(15)** ...... than cooking. Indeed she had no formal cookery training **(16)** ...... she began writing on the subject in a daily newspaper in 1969. Delia writes simple step-by-step recipes **(17)** ...... even inexperienced cooks can follow. What's **(18)** ...... her recipes are tried-and-tested, Delia has made them successfully **(19)** ...... least twenty times before they appear on television or in one of her books.

Because people trust Delia's recipes, they tend to take her advice **(20)** ...... large numbers. In 1998, after Delia presented three programmes devoted **(21)** ...... the cooking of eggs, sales of eggs in Britain increased by fifty-four million. Similarly, sales of cranberries increased by thirty percent after Delia included **(22)** ...... of the little red berries in a recipe for cooking roast duck. In supermarkets across the country, shoppers were demanding cranberries, **(23)** ...... unfortunately there were none left to buy.

Cooking is not Delia's only interest, **(24)** .... She is also a director of her local football club, where she runs a restaurant at the ground.

Part 3

For questions **25–34**, read the text below. Use the word given in capitals at the end of some of the lines to form a word that fits the gap **in the same line**. There is an example at the beginning **(0)**.

In the exam you write your answers IN CAPITAL LETTERS on a separate answer sheet.

Example: | **0** | S | P | E | C | T | A | C | U | L | A | R |

Young artists on display

Tip Strip

Question 25: Both a prefix and a suffix are needed here.

Question 31: A prefix is needed here, but it's not a negative one.

Question 33: Which suffix is needed to make an adjective from this noun?

The road to Elgol on the Isle of Skye provides one of the most

(0) ...... and beautiful journeys in Scotland. It was an   **SPECTACLE**

(25) ...... clear and lovely day when I travelled there to see   **SPECIAL**

an **(26)** ...... of paintings by local primary school children.   **EXHIBIT**

The **(27)** ...... designed school overlooks the sea, just next to   **TRADITION**

the little harbour from which fishermen and boatloads of

(28) ...... set out. From the playground the children have   **TOUR**

(29) ...... views of the nearby Cuillin Mountains and the   **WONDER**

gigantic cliffs along the seashore.

That the children take **(30)** ...... in their local environment is   **PROUD**

evident in their art work. I saw some very fine landscapes

on display, and in the booklet of artists' profiles produced

to **(31)** ...... the show, several of the young artists expressed   **COMPANY**

their interest in either the local landscape or the sea. Each

child had chosen a **(32)** ...... piece to be framed, and these   **FAVOUR**

made a very **(33)** ...... display. Not surprisingly, all the   **EFFECT**

framed paintings were soon bought by **(34)** ...... visitors   **ENTHUSIAST**

to the school.

Part 4

For questions **35–42**, complete the second sentence so that it has a similar meaning to the first sentence, using the word given. **Do not change the word given.** You must use between **two** and **five** words, including the word given. Here is an example **(0)**.

Example:

0   What type of music do you like best?

FAVOURITE

What .... type of music?

The space can be filled by the words 'is your favourite', so you write:

Example:	**0**	IS YOUR FAVOURITE

In the exam you write only the missing words IN CAPITAL LETTERS on a separate answer sheet.

Tip Strip

Question 36: You need to make the passive construction here.

Question 39: 'unlikely' is an adjective, so needs a form of the verb 'to be' before it.

Question 41: Which word combines with 'better' to express an obligation?

35 Denise always keeps her mobile switched on because David may need to contact her.

CASE

Denise never switches her mobile .... needs to contact her.

36 A man at the museum entrance gave us a map.

GIVEN

We .... a man at the museum entrance.

37 'Don't touch the plate, it's very hot,' the waitress said to me.

NOT

The waitress .... the plate because it was very hot.

38 Chris doesn't type as fast as his secretary.

TYPIST

Chris' secretary is .... than he is.

39 This cold weather probably won't last for more than a week.

UNLIKELY

This cold weather ……………… for more than a week.

40 It isn't easy for Zoe to answer the telephone in Spanish.

DIFFICULTY

Zoe ……………… the telephone in Spanish.

41 'I have a plane to catch, so I ought to leave the party early,' said Fiona.

BETTER

I have a plane to catch, so I ……………… the party early.

42 Patty remembered to pack everything except her toothbrush.

FORGOT

The only thing which ……………… her toothbrush.

TEST 3: LISTENING

You will hear people talking in eight different situations. For questions **1–8**, choose the best answer (**A**, **B** or **C**).

Tip Strip

Question 2: Read the question and the three options before listening. Can you predict which one is the correct answer? Listen and see if you were right.

Question 4: A number of skills are mentioned, but only one is essential when you apply for the job.

Question 5: Read the question carefully. You have to listen for what is attracting customers now, not what may attract them in the future.

1   You hear a woman talking about the final episode of a TV series.

   What does she say about it?

   A   It wasn't as good as previous episodes.

   B   It failed to attract a large number of viewers.

   C   It delivered an unexpected end to the story.

   | 1 |

2   You hear a DJ who works in a club, talking about his job.

   What makes him unhappy?

   A   being asked to play old-fashioned types of music

   B   being asked to play the same track more than once

   C   being asked to play the bands which he dislikes most

   | 2 |

3   You hear a man talking about an art exhibition.

   What does he criticise about it?

   A   the way the paintings were displayed

   B   the number of paintings in the exhibition

   C   the lack of information about the paintings

   | 3 |

4   You hear a radio announcement about a job vacancy.

   What skill must you have if you want the job?

   A   an ability to deal with complaints

   B   an ability to work with numbers

   C   an ability to write well

   | 4 |

5   You hear part of an interview with a restaurant owner.

What is attracting customers to the restaurant?

A   a website

B   magazine reviews

C   personal recommendations

5

6   You hear part of a talk by a young man who's just come back from a trip.

What was the main benefit of the trip for him?

A   He became more independent.

B   He learnt a foreign language.

C   He made new friends.

6

7   On the radio, you hear a sports journalist talking about an article she has written.

What is the article about?

A   the history of sport

B   the benefits of sport

C   the lack of sports facilities

7

8   You hear a young man giving a talk about going camping.

What is his advice?

A   take a good variety of foodstuffs

B   go prepared for bad weather

C   choose the area carefully

8

Part 2

You will hear a radio programme about the history of roller skating. For questions **9–18**, complete the sentences.

History of roller skating

Tip Strip

Question 12: You need to write the full name of the ballet. Be careful with your spelling.

Question 14: Listen for the name of a sport. If it consists of two words, remember you will not get a mark if you write only one.

Question 18: What type of word are you listening for? You need the comparative form of two adjectives here.

The country where the first roller skates were probably made was

9

In 1760, John Merlin went to a ball in London playing a

10 whilst on roller skates.

Unfortunately, John Merlin injured himself when he broke a

11 at the ball.

In Germany, roller skating was used in a ballet called

12

James Plimpton's invention helped roller skaters to control the

13 of their skates.

The first team sport to be played on roller skates was

14

In Detroit in 1937, the first **15** in the sport

took place.

The use of plastics meant that both the _and_ **16** of

roller skates improved.

The musical _Starlight Express_ was seen by as many as

17 in London.

The speaker says that modern roller skates are now

and **18** than ever before.

Part 3

You will hear five different students talking about their first year at university. For questions **19–23**, choose from the list (**A–F**) what each student says. Use the letters only once. There is one extra letter which you do not need to use.

Tip Strip

A: One of the speakers mentions people who made unfavourable comments about their chosen subject. Listen for these negative views.

B: Speakers 3 and 5 mention having a job while studying, but who is talking about the present?

F: Speakers 1, 3 and 5 mention student parties and outings. Which speaker is enjoying them now?

A I had to face some criticism when I chose a subject to study.

Speaker 1   **19**

B I was able to change an earlier decision about my studies.

Speaker 2   **20**

C I'm pleased that I'm able to combine studying with a job.

Speaker 3   **21**

D I had to be careful when choosing which college to study at.

Speaker 4   **22**

E I had to give up a good job to concentrate on my studies.

Speaker 5   **23**

F I'm happy to have an active social life while at college.

Part 4

You will hear an interview with the film actor Mikey Standish. For questions **24–30**, choose the best answer (**A**, **B** or **C**).

Tip Strip

Question 25: Underline the three words that express feelings. Did Mikey regret accepting the job? What made him feel slightly frightened?

Question 28: This is a long introductory sentence. Underline the key words (recommends … go to drama school … because) to focus your attention. Why is drama good for them?

Question 30: The word 'immediate' is very important here. Mikey has lots of plans, but you need to listen for what he wants to do next, not next year.

24 Mikey feels it is unfair when people suggest that

    A some types of role are unsuitable for him.
    B he's trying to imitate other well-known actors.
    C he always plays rather similar characters.

| 24 |

25 How did Mikey feel while playing the character called Simon?

    A sorry that he had decided to accept it
    B unsure about Simon's character
    C worried that Simon was so similar to himself

| 25 |

26 What kind of role does Mikey now refuse to play?

    A weak people who become heroes
    B the male lead in romantic films
    C characters who do not change at all

| 26 |

27 Why did Mikey decide to go to drama school?

    A It had been a long-held ambition.
    B He felt he had no other option.
    C A film director suggested it.

| 27 |

28 Mikey recommends that young people interested in acting go to drama school because

    A it allows them to compare their skills with others.
    B it teaches them to be competitive in the real world.
    C it helps them decide whether acting is right for them.

| 28 |

29 What does Mikey say about his celebrity status?

    A It was hard to get used to at first.
    B It's making him increasingly uncomfortable.
    C It has tended to come about gradually.

| 29 |

30 What are Mikey's immediate plans for the future?

    A to take a break from film acting
    B to write the script for a film
    C to direct a film himself

| 30 |

Part 1 (3 minutes)

Answer these questions:

Do you work or do you study?

Can you tell us something about the place where you study or work?

What type of work would you like to do in the future?

Part 2 (3 or 4 minutes)

People and animals (compare, contrast and speculate)

Turn to pictures 1 and 2 on page 130, which show people and animals.

Candidate A, compare and contrast these photographs, and say how the people and the animals may be feeling. You have a minute to do this.

Candidate B, do you like animals?

Music (compare, contrast and speculate)

Turn to pictures 1 and 2 on page 131 which show people playing different instruments.

Candidate B, compare and contrast these photographs, and say how much the people may be enjoying the experience. You have a minute to do this.

Candidate A, can you play an instrument?

Part 3 (3 or 4 minutes)

Looking after our environment (discuss and evaluate)

Turn to the pictures on page 132, which show different ways in which people can look after their environment. Imagine that you have to give a talk to a group of young children about the importance of a clean environment.

Which pictures would you choose to talk about? Why?

Which picture would you choose for a poster about your talk? Why?

Part 4 (3 or 4 minutes)

Answer these questions:

How easy is it to recycle things in your area?

What school subjects teach you about the environment?

What is the easiest thing we can do to look after the environment?

Part 1

You are going to read a magazine article about the Institute of Modern Music in Brighton (BIMM). For questions **1–8**, choose the answer (**A**, **B**, **C** or **D**) which you think fits best according to the text.

The Brighton Institute of Modern Music, also known as BIMM, recently doubled in size with the opening of BIMM West. Jarvis Cocker, Kaiser Chiefs, the Young Knives and Scissor Sisters are among those who have addressed students, and various shaky *YouTube* clips exist of drum course members playing along with Chad Smith of the Red Hot Chili Peppers.

The original BIMM, now called BIMM East, opened in 2002, after Bruce Dickinson, guitarist with the Little Angels, often in the charts in the 1990s, decided to move from running the Academy of Contemporary Music in Guildford, and set up something closer to his own heart. 'We have a more specialist niche here: we're more band, more rock'n'roll oriented. Guildford's a really good school, but we don't do music IT here – we want the substance, we look after the band oriented people. We own it, and we set the culture, and that's great,' says Bruce.

Indeed, the streets of Brighton and Hove now throng with young people carrying guitar backpacks who are heading to classes. Courses range from one-year diplomas to BA honours degrees, with students specialising in guitar, bass, drums or vocals, or focussing on the touring and management end of things. While the strings and percussion departments are male-dominated, two-thirds of the singers are female.

'The biggest myth musicians have is that someone will wave a magic wand and sort out the business side. Bands who make it actually accept responsibility for all aspects of what goes on,' says Dickinson. So, no matter what the student's speciality, their courses will include business modules. The story of popular music is riddled with footnotes about artists being
40 ripped off by shiny-suited managers. They are the people who produce contracts that you need a microscope to read and who retire to the
43 Bahamas while their cash cows remain as poor as ever.

'There's a live performance workshop every week, for which students are given a song to learn,' says Jim Williams, head of the guitar department. 'You'd expect something heavy, by,

say, System of a Down to be the most popular track, but last year it was a Norah Jones song, really delicate, that people seemed to like the most. They were dreading it, but they were so pleased to get it right.'

Those weekly performances involve individuals from various disciplines being matched together, and that's how Floors and Walls became a unit last year, with singer Alex Adams hooking up with guitar, bass and drum contemporaries. 'I was into drum'n'bass and garage. Through some friends I heard about BIMM. As a singer, it's been fantastic: you learn technical exercises, warming up, keeping the voice healthy, the history of music, but the main thing for me is the live performance events. Learn a song, and then you're at a proper venue with a band. It's a place where you're all in the same boat, and it's competitive, but in a friendly way.'

The competition element peaks in the quest to appear on the annual compilation CD: last year, 160 demos were sent in by students hoping to make the final cut of twelve. The BIMM principal, Vaseema Hamilton, is particularly pleased when diploma students' tracks show up on the CD. 'Most of the students are full-time and from local schools,' she says. 'They are often people who didn't really engage with school. You
78 know they might end up quite disengaged from life otherwise, and it's great when they get on to the album and sound better than some of those from higher levels.'

Tutors, too, are on a learning curve. Members of staff undertake a two-year, part-time special teaching course at Sussex University. 'It's a bit like a football team here, with people fulfilling different roles,' says Dickinson. 'You've got your tutors who can transcribe the entire back catalogue of Frank Zappa, and then you've got your less academic but very vociferous types.'
91 There's a constant turnover, with many going on the road, on tour to all sorts of places. Students like that – it shows them the facts of life as a musician. One thing is clear to all who come to BIMM: it moves in its own way, and there is something quite magical about it.

Tip Strip

Question 2: What does Dickinson mean by 'We own it, and we set the culture'?

Question 5: What is 'the main thing' for Alex Adams?

Question 8: There is a constant turnover of what? Look at the previous line.

1   In the first paragraph, the writer mentions a number of famous artists in order to

   A   show that BIMM relies too much on big names.
   B   emphasise that BIMM is held in high regard.
   C   compare the artists' relative importance.
   D   win the support of BIMM students.

2   Bruce Dickinson likes his job at BIMM better than his previous job because he is now able to

   A   concentrate on training band leaders.
   B   attract students from other colleges.
   C   decide about the content of the courses.
   D   be amongst the best of the chart-toppers.

3   What does the expression 'ripped off' in line 40 mean?

   A   cheated
   B   attacked
   C   persuaded
   D   impressed

4   The words 'cash cows' in line 43 refer to

   A   managers.
   B   contracts.
   C   students.
   D   artists.

5   Alex Adams says that what he appreciates most about BIMM is

   A   the prestige of the degrees it awards.
   B   the opportunity to perform professionally.
   C   the mixture of styles it embraces.
   D   the way it looks after artists' well-being.

6   The BIMM principal, Vaseema Hamilton, uses the expression 'end up quite disengaged from life' (line 78) to indicate that some students

   A   come from broken homes.
   B   fail to appear on the BIMM CD.
   C   make more of an effort than others.
   D   need special support to succeed.

7   Dickinson compares BIMM to a football club to suggest that members of staff

   A   want to encourage healthy competition.
   B   like travelling to represent the college.
   C   take on a number of different roles.
   D   are very loyal to their institution.

8   The word 'many' in line 91 refers to

   A   tutors.
   B   facts.
   C   students.
   D   places.

You are going to read a magazine article about an African musician. Seven sentences have been removed from the article. Choose from the sentences **A–H** the one which fits each gap (**9–15**). There is one extra sentence which you do not need to use.

Femi Kuti, a great African musician

In the fashion-led world of pop culture, carrying a famous name is always a burden, as the offspring of musicians like John Lennon and Bob Marley have found. Yet the history of much of the world's music – certainly in Africa – is based on a long and deep tradition of passing on the torch from one generation to the next. Femi Kuti is the son of Fela Kuti, a renowned musician who died ten years ago.

Throughout his career, Femi Kuti has had to suffer comparisons with his father. You can't fill the boots of a legend and Fela Kuti was not only an extraordinary and innovative musician but one of the giants of world music. **9** He has kept alive the flame of Afro-beat as well as bringing his own unique creativity to its rhythms.

Femi was born in London in 1962, when his father was a student at the Royal Academy. Fela never showed his oldest son any signs of approval or encouragement. **10** Yet by the age of fifteen, Femi's impressive playing had earned him a place in his father's band, *Egypt 80*, on merit.

Femi didn't have to wait long for his first opportunity to head that band. In 1985, it had been booked to play at the Hollywood Bowl, but Femi's father failed to make it on to the plane. **11** This gave him the confidence he needed to start a band of his own.

In 1986, together with keyboard player Dele Sosimi, Femi left his father's band and formed the band *Positive Force*, resulting in tensions between father and son that were to last several years. **12** Now a collector's item, its mix of funk, soul and jazz, driven by thundering percussion, proved that he could stand on his own two feet.

Femi made his first US tour in 1995, which culminated in an acclaimed appearance at the Summer stage in New York's Central Park in July. The tour coincided with the release of his album, *Femi Kuti*, which earned him very good reviews across Europe and the US. **13** He finally admitted that his son had what it takes.

Though Femi remains resentful of what he sees as his father's lack of support early in his career, he recognises that he learnt things from him: ' **14** ,' says Femi. That individuality was certainly evident on his next album, *Shoki Shoki*, which added fresh flavours drawn from contemporary R&B and dance music.

His latest album, *Live at the Shrine*, was recorded in 2004 at the club in Lagos which remains the centre of his operations and where he continues to play every Sunday night when he's not on tour. And as we wait for his next album, the Kuti tradition continues and Femi's own son now plays alongside him in *Positive Force*. **15** Femi sounds proud of his son.

Tip Strip

Question 9: The sentence before the gap is full of praise for Femi Kuti's father. You need a sentence which links this to his son's successful career.

Question 11: What did Femi do when his father failed to turn up?

Question 13: The sentence after the gap refers to Femi's father. Sentences B, C, F and H mention his father. Which one is the correct answer?

A Femi stepped forward to fill his place, and did so, by all accounts, with considerable skill.

B It also won him six awards at Nigeria's Fame Music Awards and led at last to a reconciliation with his father.

C Yet his father's long shadow should not obscure the fact that Femi Kuti has developed into a fine performer in his own right.

D It was at this place that he helped to fund a variety of cultural, social and educational projects.

E Femi's debut album with the new band, *No Cause for Alarm?*, was recorded in Lagos and released on Polygram Nigeria in 1987.

F The one thing I learned from my father was to be true to myself, and that's the advice I've given my own child.

G After giving him a saxophone as a young boy, he then refused to give him any lessons.

H When I look at his life, it's very hard for me to be angry with him because he taught me to be different and to do things my own way.

You are going to read a magazine article about people who have taken up dangerous sports. For questions **16–30**, choose from the people (**A–D**). The people may be chosen more than once.

A	**Brenda Gordon**
B	**Guy Stanton**
C	**Debbie Bridge**
D	**Max Wainright**

Tip Strip

Question 18: Find a similar way of saying 'was confident'.

Question 22: Which person was told by a teacher not to do something?

Question 26: Find a similar way of saying a 'feeling of joy'.

Which person

was aware of making a mistake during training?	16
expected the first day of training to be relatively easy?	17
was confident of having the physical strength to succeed?	18
improved their performance by following some useful advice?	19
realised their co-trainees had had some experience in a related sport?	20
mentions having gained considerable confidence since starting?	21
was warned not to try to use skills acquired in other sports?	22
believes the training venue used is the best available?	23
is confident of overcoming any feelings of fear?	24
felt nervous when preparing to try out the sport for the first time?	25
mentions the feeling of joy that the sport gave?	26
was told the sport was not as dangerous as people think?	27
was more successful than somebody else in a first attempt?	28
felt disappointed when the trainer gave an order to stop?	29
felt uncomfortable with their appearance on arriving for a lesson?	30

Anyone for extreme sports?

Tired of going to the gym? Why not try something you might actually enjoy? Four courageous people describe their own choices …

Brenda Gordon: flying trapeze   I wanted to do something where I was having so much fun I wouldn't even notice I was exercising at all. I decided to try out a half-day circus-skills course. It all started with a series of preparation exercises. Then I stood facing the flying trapeze, and all of a sudden I noticed a slight fluttering in my stomach. Next I was shown the right way to grip the trapeze and how to step off the platform without hitting my back. Then, suddenly, I was being counted down from three. My heart was racing but I kept thinking I'd no doubt be able to take my body weight in my very muscular arms. Then in a moment I'd stepped off and, incredibly, I was swinging through the air. I was aware of a real feeling of regret when the instructor told me to stop. That was a year ago, and I am now a fearless trapeze flyer, though my muscles still hurt after each and every session.

Guy Stanton: ice climbing   I had my first ice-climbing lesson at an indoor climbing centre which has an enormous artificial ice cave. I turned up fully kitted-up in heavy climbing boots with sharp-toothed metal crampons, and armed with two metal ice axes, which was embarrassing as my co-trainees all expected to get their gear from the centre. The instructor ran through a demonstration. Then it was my turn. I buried the axes on the ice, kicked one boot at the wall, then the other, and started climbing. But I had forgotten my first important lesson: don't bury your axes too deep. As my desire not to fall increased, so I hammered them deeper until they got stuck. My arms were aching and I stopped, utterly disappointed with myself. The trainer shouted some encouragement: 'You can do it, don't grip the axes so hard!' I did so and my more relaxed style meant less pressure on my arms, so I started enjoying it. I still feel frightened when I'm high up, but I know I'll feel completely at ease eventually.

Debbie Bridge: freediving   Freediving is a sport which consists of diving to great depths without an oxygen tank. I took part in a freediving course organised by a leading sub-aqua website. This is surely the best place in the world to learn this skill. My training took place in a 30-metre high and 6-metre wide cylindrical water tank. Unlike me, who had never been deeper than the swimming-pool floor, my co-trainees were all scuba divers. Our trainer was keen to prove freediving is not so risky. 'When practised correctly, it is a very safe sport,' she said. After a few lectures about safety, and suitably kitted with flippers and a diving mask, I was ready to get into the water. With a partner, we were going to attempt to descend and ascend by pulling on a rope. My partner dived first but had trouble and stopped at 5 metres. Then I dived, pulling myself downwards on the rope and reached 15 metres easily, feeling more and more at ease. This sport is not about adrenaline but about being calm.

Max Wainright: snowboarding   I'd always wanted to try snowboarding, so I went for a training day at an indoor snow slope near my home – a 170-metre-long slope, all covered by 1500 tonnes of man-made snow which is surprisingly like the real thing. Having had the pleasure of learning the basics of snowboarding several years before in the French Alps, I'd hoped that returning to the sport might be a bit like riding a bike, something you supposedly never forget. But it seemed that most of what I'd learned had melted away just like snow. I knew I shouldn't use the techniques I'd learnt in years of surfing and skiing, and I didn't. My instructor had said they were not applicable to snowboarding at all. I started riding slowly at first, and couldn't get the balance right. It took hours before I could pick up speed and successfully perform a neat turn. But I was getting the hang of this! What a thrill to feel the cool air rushing by, what fun to crash into the snow!

TEST 4: WRITING

You **must** answer this question. Write your answer in **120–150** words in an appropriate style.

1   You have received an email from an English-speaking friend, Patrick, who wants to find a summer job in your country. Read Patrick's email and the notes you have made. Then write an email to Patrick, using **all** your notes.

---

email   Page 1 of 1

From: Patrick Moody
Sent: 30th October 2008
Subject: Summer job

I'd love to spend the summer working in your country. I think I could learn a lot! Do you think it would help me improve my knowledge of your language? — definitely!

give details of jobs —
I have some experience of summer jobs in supermarkets and last year I worked in a restaurant all summer. What summer jobs might be available in your area?

I would not expect to earn a lot of money, of course, but do you think I'd earn enough to pay for my expenses? — only basic expenses …

No, another friend staying, but I'll find … —
Finally, If I get a job, would it be possible to stay in your house?

Please write soon.

Regards,

Patrick

Write your **email**. You must use grammatically correct sentences with accurate spelling and punctuation in a style appropriate for the situation.

Tip Strip
Question 1

Have you included these points?

1 how it could help him improve his language

2 some jobs and why you would think they are good or bad

3 that wages are not very good, but enough for expenses

4 that somebody else is in your spare room, but you will try to find accommodation for him (e.g. friends, youth hostel)

Part 2

Write an answer to **one** of the questions 2–4 in this part. Write an answer in **120–180** words in an appropriate style.

Tip Strip

Question 2

Have you included these points?

1 why you want to attend the course (mention your enthusiasm and willingness to work for hours)

2 a description of your musical skills and experience; what your favourite music is

Question 3

Remember the main purpose of a review is to give a personal opinion. You must give the reader a clear impression of the quality of what you are reviewing.

1 Explain what the cartoon or cartoon characters are like.

2 Say what makes it funny and give reasons why it may or may not appeal to older people.

Question 4: Use narrative and description to say what happened to Harry. Remember some things have to be positive because at the end, Harry thinks it had been one of the best days in his life. Why was this?

Question 5(a): Decide whether it is or it isn't, and include details of plot, characters, events, message, style, etc, to back up your opinions.

Question 5(b): Explain in what way the plot and the characters are thrilling/interesting. Remember your friend wants to read the book, so don't say how it all ends!

2 You have seen an advertisement for a music course and you want to apply.

> **Are you good at writing songs, or at singing or at playing an intrument?**
>
> At the Heath College of Music we are looking for new talent!
> We are offering four free places on our summer courses.
> We are looking for enthusiastic people who are willing to devote many hours a day to studying. Write to Clara Barnes, the director, explaining
> * why you would want to attend a course,
> * what musical skills you have,
> * and what your favourite music is.

Write your **letter of application**. Do not write any postal addresses.

3 You recently saw this notice in the local newspaper.

> **Do you watch a cartoon which is not just for children?**
>
> Write us a review of the cartoon for the college magazine. Describe some of the characters and say what makes it funny and if you think older people like it too.
>
> The best review will be published next month!

Write your **review**.

4 Your teacher has asked you to write a story for an international magazine. The story must **end** with the following words:

Despite everything that had happened, Harry thought this had been one of the best days in his life.

Write your **story**.

5 Answer **one** of the following two questions based on your reading of **one** of these set books.

(a) Author – *Name of book*
Is this one of the best novels you have ever read? Write a **review** for the college magazine saying whether it is or it isn't, giving reasons and examples from the book to back up your opinions.

(b) Author – *Name of book*

> *I want to read a novel with a thrilling plot and interesting characters. Can you recommend one? Peter*

Write a **letter** to Peter recommending the book and saying in what ways the plot and the characters are interesting.

Part 1

For questions **1–12**, read the text below and decide which answer (**A**, **B**, **C** or **D**) best fits each gap. There is an example at the beginning **(0)**.

In the exam you mark your answers on a separate answer sheet.

Example:

0 A puts   **B** sets   **C** places   **D** fetches

Lunch is for sharing

Tip Strip
Question 1: Which is the correct word in the context of the Internet?
Question 9: Which of these linkers is usually followed by a comma?
Question 12: Which of these words is usually followed by the preposition 'on'?

Mimi Ito carefully **(0)** ....together her children's packed lunches each morning. She then photographs them on her cameraphone and **(1)** ...... the pictures on her online blog. In this way, Mimi is able to **(2)** ...... a record of meals that she is **(3)** ...... of, and hungry websurfers **(4)** ...... the chance to look at her mouth-watering creations. For these are no ordinary lunches, Mimi prepares what are **(5)** ...... as bento meals for her children.

A bento is a single-portion Japanese takeaway meal that traditionally **(6)** ...... of rice, fish or meat, with vegetables on the side. In Japan, they are normally served in distinctive trays divided into sections for the different parts of the meal. Mimi thinks that children in **(7)** ...... enjoy having small compartments with little bits of food that are **(8)** ...... to their small appetites. **(9)** ...... , if we think of the excitement that many of us feel when our airline meal arrives, it's **(10)** ...... to understand the fascination.

Mimi was born in Japan and currently lives in the USA. She is fairly health **(11)** ...... , but believes that having wide tastes and finding pleasure in food is important. She thinks that it's possible to **(12)** ...... on that whilst at the same time also eating healthily.

0	**A** puts	**B** sets	**C** places	**D** fetches
1	**A** mails	**B** sends	**C** posts	**D** delivers
2	**A** hold	**B** keep	**C** save	**D** do
3	**A** content	**B** satisfied	**C** proud	**D** pleased
4	**A** take	**B** get	**C** gain	**D** find
5	**A** titled	**B** called	**C** named	**D** known
6	**A** consists	**B** includes	**C** contains	**D** involves
7	**A** specific	**B** particular	**C** special	**D** precise
8	**A** suited	**B** fitted	**C** created	**D** designed
9	**A** Whatever	**B** Despite	**C** Regardless	**D** However
10	**A** simple	**B** clear	**C** easy	**D** plain
11	**A** sensible	**B** conscious	**C** knowledgeable	**D** informed
12	**A** focus	**B** emphasise	**C** stress	**D** aim

For questions **13–24**, read the text below and think of the word which best fits each gap. Use only **one** word in each gap. There is an example at the beginning **(0)**.

In the exam you write your answers IN CAPITAL LETTERS on a separate answer sheet.

Example: | 0 | | O | N | E | | | | | | | |

Mr Bean

Tip Strip

Question 13: Which preposition is needed here?

Question 18: A contrastive linker is needed here.

Question 24: Which word combines with 'as' to mean 'for example'?

The comedy character Mr Bean is **(0)** ...... of Britain's most successful exports. The original television show, only half-an-hour **(13)** ...... length, was first broadcast in 1990. **(14)** ...... then, the fourteen episodes of the show have been shown on **(15)** ...... than two hundred TV stations around the world, as **(16)** ...... as on fifty airlines. The film, *Mr Bean's Holiday* was a global smash hit and the character, played **(17)** ...... the actor Rowan Atkinson, is instantly recognisable to millions of people around the world.

So why is Mr Bean so popular? **(18)** ...... many people regard Mr Bean as a typically British character, the initial inspiration actually came from a French comic character known **(19)** ...... Monsieur Hulot, created by the French comedian Jacques Tati.

According **(20)** ...... Rowan Atkinson, however, the actual character of Mr Bean is mostly based on **(21)** ...... own personality as a nine-year-old. Mr Bean is a man **(22)** ...... is awkward, self-conscious and accident-prone. He is very selfish and doesn't really understand very much about the world **(23)** ...... him. He is really a child in a man's body. This, as Atkinson explains, is the basis for a lot of visual comedy and he mentions comedians **(24)** ...... as Charlie Chaplin and Stan Laurel as other famous examples.

Part 3

For questions **25–34**, read the text below. Use the word given in capitals at the end of some of the lines to form a word that fits the gap **in the same line**. There is an example at the beginning **(0)**.

In the exam you write your answers IN CAPITAL LETTERS on a separate answer sheet

Example: | **0** | A | R | T | I | S | T | I | C | | | |

Computer games

Tip Strip

Question 26: Is a noun or an adjective needed here?

Question 29: Which suffix is needed to make a word which means 'people who make music'?

Question 33: How can we make this adjective negative?

To get an idea of the **(0)** ...... and technical skill that goes   **ARTIST**

Into a computer game, you only need to visit the Los Angeles

studio of Electronic Arts, the world's largest and most **(25)** ......   **INFLUENCE**

gamemaker. The firm's **(26)** ...... team have just started work   **CREATE**

on the latest version of one of their most popular games. As you

enter the building, you see an **(27)** ...... display of photographs   **IMPRESS**

that help you to imagine what the game's particular look and

style will be like.

The **(28)** ...... of the game will involve engineers, technical   **DEVELOP**

experts and **(29)** ...... , and will cost more than $10 million.   **MUSIC**

These days, there is a great deal of **(30)** ...... between   **SIMILAR**

making a game and making a Hollywood movie, and it's big

business.

According to **(31)** ...... , Americans spend more than $70   **ECONOMY**

billion on computer games each year, or in other words,

they buy two games per household. Part of the **(32)** ...... for   **EXPLAIN**

the success of the games is the **(33)** ...... rise in the number of   **EXPECTED**

adults who are buying them, not as gifts for teenagers, but for

their own **(34)** ...... use.   **PERSON**

Part 4

For questions **35–42**, complete the second sentence so that it has a similar meaning to the first sentence, using the word given. **Do not change the word given.** You must use between **two** and **five** words, including the word given. Here is an example **(0)**.

Example:

0 What type of music do you like best?

FAVOURITE

What .... type of music?

The gap can be filled by the words 'is your favourite', so you write:

Example: | **0** | IS YOUR FAVOURITE |

In the exam you write only the missing words IN CAPITAL LETTERS on a separate answer sheet.

Tip Strip

Question 37: You need to use the adjective in this sentence.

Question 41: Which phrasal verb means to say no to an offer?

Question 42: A personal pronoun is needed before 'ambition'.

35 Which of the places you visited interested you most?

THE

Which was .... that you visited?

36 Sally arrived late at the conference because her flight was delayed.

TIME

If Sally's .... , she wouldn't have arrived late at the conference.

37 The happy couple expressed their thanks for all the presents they had received.

GRATEFUL

The happy couple said that .... all the presents they had received.

38 Colin will only read your email if you mark it as urgent.

UNLESS

Colin will .... you mark it as urgent.

39 Tania regrets lending her new laptop to her little brother.

WISHES

Tania .... her new laptop to her little brother.

40 I'm sure it was a real disappointment for Gerry that his team didn't win promotion.

BEEN

Gerry .... that his team didn't win promotion.

41 Alex offered Cindy a lift on his new motorbike, but she didn't accept.

TURNED

Cindy .... offer of a lift on his new motorbike.

42 I always wanted to be a professional dancer.

AMBITION

It was .... be a professional dancer.

Part 1

You will hear people talking in eight different situations. For questions **1–8**, choose the best answer (**A**, **B** or **C**).

1   You hear part of a programme about music in schools.

     Why are fewer children joining school choirs?

     A   They are unwilling to sing in public.

     B   Their parents don't encourage them to sing.

     C   Their teachers lack the necessary musical skills.

     | | 1 |

2   You overhear a conversation about evening classes.

     Why did the girl decide to register for a photography course?

     A   She wanted to take better holiday snaps.

     B   She thought it would help her in her career.

     C   She needed a relaxing change from her studies.

     | | 2 |

3   You overhear two people talking about a new café.

     What did they both approve of?

     A   the size of the portions

     B   the originality of the food

     C   the efficiency of the service

     | | 3 |

4   You hear a man talking about exploring underground caves.

     What is he?

     A   an experienced caver

     B   a journalist

     C   a student

     | | 4 |

5 You overhear a woman talking about a job interview she had.

What does she say about it?

A   Some of the questions were unfair.

B   She felt she was insufficiently prepared.

C   The interviewers put her under pressure.

| | 5 |

6 You overhear a woman talking about a language course.

What does she criticise about it?

A   There are too many students.

B   Grammar isn't focussed on.

C   It isn't challenging enough.

| | 6 |

7 On the radio, you hear a man talking about food.

What does he do?

A   He's a shop owner.

B   He's a cookery writer.

C   He's a chef in a restaurant.

| | 7 |

8 You hear a man talking about moving house.

How did he feel after moving to a new area?

A   worried that he wouldn't see his old friends

B   concerned about how his children would adapt

C   surprised by how welcoming his new neighbours were

| | 8 |

Part 2

You will hear a radio programme about a day in the life of a television researcher. For questions **9–18**, complete the sentences.

TV researcher

Tip Strip

Question 10: The subject consists of two words. You need to write both of them correctly.

Question 13: Listen for another way of saying 'a sort of'.

Question 16: You can try and predict the answer here. What do you think Jamie could use to help him see the crocodiles?

The subject that Rita studied first at university was

[_____ **9**]

Before getting her present job, Rita studied a subject called

[_____ **10**]

On the day she tells us about, the country where Rita was working was

[_____ **11**]

There were a total of [_____ **12**]

people in Rita's team on that day.

The animal which Jamie had to photograph was a sort of

[_____ **13**]

The camera crew had to film Jamie as he climbed over the edge of a

[_____ **14**]

Rita's lunch consisted of sandwiches with

[_____ **15**] inside.

Jamie had to hold a [_____ **16**]

to help him see the crocodiles as he crossed a river.

A special light which the crew was using, known as a

[_____ **17**] , stopped working.

Rita says that Jamie looks really [_____ **18**]

when you see him crossing the river on the programme.

Part 3

You will hear five different craft workers giving advice to people who want to start a home-based business to sell the things they make. For questions **19–23**, choose from the list (**A–F**) what advice each speaker gives. Use the letters only once. There is one extra letter which you do not need to use.

Tip Strip

A: Advertising is mentioned by speakers 1, 4 and 5, but only one of them recommends advertising locally.

F: Which speaker believes it is necessary to plan the financial aspects of the business in advance?

D: Listen for a speaker who likes a tidy studio to work in.

A expand your business by advertising locally

Speaker 1 ☐ **19**

B continue to learn in order to perfect your product

Speaker 2 ☐ **20**

C employ family and friends to market your product

Speaker 3 ☐ **21**

D spend time organising your workspace properly

Speaker 4 ☐ **22**

E increase business by selling online

Speaker 5 ☐ **23**

F produce a clear marketing plan for your business

Part 4

You will hear an interview with Monica Darcey, who has written a bestselling book about gardening. For questions **24–30**, choose the best answer (**A**, **B** or **C**).

Tip Strip

Question 24: Monica tells us what large numbers of her readers do. Do they get good results?

Question 25: Monica mentions a problem with her health. Was this the reason why her parents were unhappy about her interest in gardening?

Question 30: Underline the word 'unsure'. It tells you that you have to listen for a reason why Monica has doubts about accepting a job on television.

24 Monica says that most people who buy her book

    A have made mistakes in gardening.
    B are knowledgeable about gardening.
    C do not trust professional gardeners.

24

25 How did Monica's parents feel about her early interest in gardening?

    A They were concerned about the effects on her health.
    B They were worried that she lacked other interests.
    C They feared her enthusiasm would affect her studies.

25

26 Monica applied to work as a gardening journalist because

    A it would give her an extra source of income.
    B she'd found the experience of writing rewarding.
    C there might be opportunities to do some research.

26

27 Why did Monica give up her job on a magazine?

    A She got an offer of work somewhere else.
    B She didn't get on with other members of staff.
    C She was not interested in the type of work she was doing.

27

28 According to Monica, what makes her gardening books special?

    A They are written in an entertaining style.
    B They are aimed at amateur enthusiasts.
    C They are the result of detailed research.

28

29 What does Monica dislike about the photographs in many gardening books?

    A They reduce the importance of the writer.
    B They help to sell poor quality writing.
    C They show an unrealistic view of their subject.

29

30 What makes Monica unsure whether to accept a job on television?

    A Her publisher may disapprove of it.
    B It may make her suddenly famous.
    C She would have less time for writing.

30

Part 1 (3 minutes)

Answer these questions:

Tell us something about your reasons for studying English.

Tell us where and how you've learnt English.

Do you know any other foreign languages?

Part 2 (3 or 4 minutes)

Transport (compare, contrast and speculate)

Turn to pictures 1 and 2 on page 133, which show people using different forms of transport.

Candidate A, compare and contrast these photographs, and say why the people may have chosen these forms of transport. You have a minute to do this.

Candidate B, do you like to travel by coach?

Games (compare, contrast and speculate)

Turn to pictures 1 and 2 on page 134, which show people playing different games.

Candidate B, compare and contrast these photographs, and say how interesting these games may be for different age groups. You have a minute to do this.

Candidate A, do you like computer games?

Part 3 (3 or 4 minutes)

Advice for foreign visitors (discuss and evaluate)

Turn to the pictures on page 135, which show information foreign visitors might need. Imagine that two young people are coming to visit this country for the first time and they want to travel on their own.

Talk about the areas where you think they definitely need advice from you, and the areas where your advice would not be so important.

Part 4 (3 or 4 minutes)

Answer these questions:

If you were visiting another country, what questions would you ask local people about safety?

Would you prefer to travel on your own or with somebody local? Why/Why not?

Would you make a trip like that if you didn't speak the local language? Why/Why not?

I made a discovery on the way to Ruth's aunt's house in Spain. The things you worry about don't always turn out as badly as you expect. Sometimes they're worse. Everything would have been different if our plane had landed on schedule. Ruth was quite nice about it, as always, but I know that she really thought it was my fault.

Our plan had been to arrive in Spain, collect the hire car, shop for groceries and still get to the house in daylight. I'd felt proud of myself when I'd booked the tickets. I'd got a special cheap offer on the Internet. But that was silly because Ruth's aunt was paying our expenses and she wasn't the kind of woman who expects people to fly on budget airlines. To her mind, you pay full price for comfort and reliability. Our flight got to Spain about three hours later than expected.

By the time we got to where our hire car was waiting amongst dozens of others, it was totally dark. The man at the desk confirmed what we'd guessed. It was too late for shopping. While I signed for the car – gripping the pen hard so that my name wouldn't look as shaky as I felt – Ruth bought two cartons of fruit juice from a vending machine.

'Ruth!' I said, as I drove cautiously out of the car park, gripping the wheel. 'Which way is it? I'm not going to be able to understand any of the road signs!'

'You just need to follow the coast road,' said
33 Ruth. 'It's simple. Things don't get tough until we take a left into the mountains.'

As all I had to do was drive straight ahead, I began to relax. Then it was time to turn off into the mountains and I un-relaxed again. Apart from anything else, you don't get street lighting on lonely country roads in southern Spain. This road climbed slowly but steadily in a series of Z-shapes, with a rocky wall on the left and a steep drop on the right. We gradually lost the rest of the traffic until there was hardly any. I can tell you now that hardly any is worse than a lot. All would be quiet and then suddenly headlights would appear behind us, sweep past us and vanish. Or lights would blaze round a corner ahead, without warning, looking as though they were coming right at us.

Ruth read out where I should go, and me and the car went. It all made sense. Or it did until she pointed to an olive grove, all silvery in the moonlight, and told me to drive into it.

'I can't,' I said. 'There's no road.'

'There's a track,' said Ruth. 'Up ahead, see? On the left. It's right opposite a white house with green shutters, just like the directions say.'

I gave way. But I wasn't happy. 'This is not a track,' I said, driving cautiously onto it. 'It's just a strip of land where the olive trees aren't.' We bounced slowly along in silence, apart from the
62 scrunching of pebbles under the wheels. Ahead was the dark outline of a small house.

'This is it,' said Ruth. 'See – we made it!'

The track opened out into a parking space beside the house. There it stopped – end of the road. 'Are you sure about this?' I whispered. 'It's really late, Ruth. If we're wrong we're going to wake people up.'

'There's no one to wake up,' said Ruth, getting out. 'The place is empty. Just waiting for us.' Somewhere in the distance, a dog barked.

Ruth was at the house. I could hear her scrabbling at the door. She turned as I reached her. 'I can't make the key work,' she said.

'I told you,' I breathed. 'We're in the wrong place.'

I went back to the car and got a torch. I thought it would show us how to put the key in. What it actually showed us was something quite different. The metal surrounding the keyhole was bright and shiny and all around it there were little marks and scratches in the old wood of the door. The lock had been changed. Very recently.

1   What does the narrator suggest about her trip in the first paragraph?

    A   She'd expected Ruth to share the blame for what happened.
    B   She'd expected Ruth to be angry with her.
    C   She'd expected aspects of it to go wrong.
    D   She'd expected her plane to be delayed.

2   What mistake did the narrator make when booking their flight?

    A   She hadn't followed Ruth's advice about the airline.
    B   She'd forgotten that someone else was paying for them.
    C   She'd chosen one that was scheduled to arrive after dark.
    D   She hadn't realised that they would need to go shopping on arrival.

3   How did the narrator feel in the car-hire office?

    A   keen not to let her nervous state show
    B   cross because she had to wait in a queue
    C   grateful for the advice of the man behind the desk
    D   confused by the documents that she needed to sign

4   'It' in line 33 refers to

    A   understanding the road signs.
    B   driving in the dark.
    C   taking a left turn.
    D   finding the way.

5   When driving into the mountains, the narrator felt

    A   reassured by the sound of passing traffic.
    B   alarmed by the sight of other car headlights.
    C   frustrated by their rather slow progress.
    D   unsure if they were on the right road.

6   How did Ruth know that they should turn into the olive grove?

    A   She was consulting a map.
    B   She had been there before.
    C   She had written instructions.
    D   She asked some local residents.

7   The word 'scrunching' in line 62 describes a type of

    A   plant.
    B   noise.
    C   movement.
    D   road surface.

8   Why couldn't the friends get into the house?

    A   The lock in the door was broken.
    B   They had brought the wrong keys.
    C   They had come to the wrong place.
    D   The keys they had didn't fit the lock.

You are going to read an extract from article about a young designer. Seven sentences have been removed from the article. Choose from the sentences **A–H** the one which fits each gap (**9–15**). There is one extra sentence which you do not need to use.

Sparkling trainers

★☆★☆★☆★☆★☆

Pauline Clifford's hobby of decorating trainers has turned into a successful business.

Pauline's hobby of customising trainers by decorating them with Swarovski crystals has grown into a fashion phenomenon. Pauline's customers send her their shoes and she decorates them with their names, favourite song lyrics, flags, or one of her own colourful designs.

Pauline is in her twenties and turns out her shoe designs in a spare room at home in Neilston, a suburban village on the outskirts of Glasgow in Scotland – a place about as far away from the red carpets, paparazzi and the glamour of celebrity land as it is possible to imagine. **9**

Pauline's company, *StarSparkles*, was formed in April 2006. Now upmarket department stores and retail chains at the fashionable end of the market are stocking her pre-customised shoes. Pauline's success isn't entirely surprising because people are keen to buy something unique. **10** And that's precisely what Pauline is offering.

So how did it all start? 'I've always liked things that are a bit different and creative,' says Pauline. 'I used to dress a bit strangely when I was growing up and I began customising things as a teenager. But it really started a couple of years back, when I bought a load of Swarovski crystals on a trip to Los Angeles. When I came back I customised some Adidas and Puma trainers.' **11** Pauline soon found herself spending all her spare time on her shoe project.

'I also emailed lots of magazines to see if they wanted to feature my shoes, and a lot of them did,' Pauline adds. Also, as she is a bit celebrity-obsessed, she found a website called *Contact Any Celebrity*, chose a few well-known people in Los Angeles, found out their shoe sizes and designed them each a pair of trainers. '**12** It was amazing.'

As the orders continued to flood in, Pauline decided to put her business on a more formal footing. **13** Pauline says: 'After I had officially been in business for about six months, I went to the Prince's Scottish Youth Business Trust. They were pretty supportive and they gave me £5000, which I used to get my website up and running, get some business cards and buy a stock of crystals.'

Pauline is negotiating to buy a stock of shoes to work on and sell internationally through her website, but she is slightly uneasy. **14** 'Some people started selling trainers similar to mine, so I had to pay for a lawyer to stop them. What I really want to do is to build up a brand name for myself, so that if anybody tries to copy me, my brand will be seen as the original and best,' she says.

'**15** But I never get bored. I definitely will have to employ someone soon – there's only so many shoes I can do. Everyone asks me if I'm not getting a bit fed up. But I love to see customers' faces when I show them their shoes. It makes me really happy, that's the best thing about it.'

A A shoe-shop manager in Glasgow saw them and ordered a few pairs to put in the shop window, and they sold straightaway.

B But who do you turn to for help when you've got a rapidly expanding enterprise on your hands and no experience of running a company?

C The well-known shops have become so like one another that it's almost impossible for the style-conscious shoe shopper to take home something that nobody else has got.

D But it was the Business Gateway organisation which helped her to draw up a business plan.

E As is the case with so many new businesses, someone else pinching and using her idea is a worry.

F It's an appropriate setting, however, for someone making their mark in footwear, because in the nineteenth century it was home to a thriving shoe industry.

G Sometimes when I'm getting behind with individual customer orders, I do get a bit stressed.

H One of them – who's a bit of a fashion icon – was photographed wearing theirs the following week, and I just couldn't believe my luck!

Part 3

You are going to read a magazine article about people who work in the tourist industry. For questions **16–30**, choose from the people (**A–E**). The people may be chosen more than once.

A	**Claire Davies**
B	**Peter Gattoni**
C	**Maria Falcon**
D	**Patrick O'Connor**
E	**Connie Ferguson**

Which person

refers to a lack of outstanding professionals in one area of work?		**16**	
stresses the need to provide clients with a balance between freedom and control?		**17**	
regrets a decision made years ago?		**18**	
mentions the need to take the right decisions under pressure?		**19**	
says people shouldn't feel discouraged if they don't earn much at first?		**20**	
gained promotion after impressing a senior colleague?		**21**	
says larger companies are able to offer better conditions to workers?		**22**	
believes that qualifications alone won't get you promotion?		**23**	
remembers making a mistake whilst doing the job?	**24**	**25**	
has been able to combine work with further study?	**26**	**27**	
looks forward to developing a new career?		**28**	
says there are likely to be more opportunities for training in the future?		**29**	
warns about the decreasing opportunities for jobs in one area?		**30**	

Thinking of a career in tourism?

The tourist industry offers a range of jobs and career opportunities. So what sort of person do you need to be to work in tourism? To begin with, you need to like people and enjoy the challenge of working in a customer focussed environment.

Claire Davies is twenty-one and is a receptionist in a five-star hotel. She says that what appeals to her most is the diversity of the challenges she faces every day – from dealing with phone calls in different languages to making bookings for restaurants. She first came to the hotel when she was on a year's work experience from university and now works part-time, which allows her to continue with her degree course in management. Her advice to anyone considering a career in hotels in not to be put off by the thought of low wages at the start. Having the right degree or diploma is no guarantee of promotion, but the right attitude and good communication skills will get you a long way.

But of course it's not just about hotels. **Peter Gattoni** is a chef in an Italian restaurant that attracts what is called the 'gourmet tourist', whose holiday is never complete without the opportunity to try out the latest dishes. Peter went straight into employment after school, but that's not something he'd recommend. 'Had I taken a full-time college course as my parents wanted, I would have made faster progress. There's a shortage of first-class chefs, so many companies are now advertising good salaries, including profit-related pay, to chefs with the right qualifications and experience, though these advantages are more likely to come from the big-name restaurants and hotel chains.'

And what about a job as a tour guide? If you enjoy communicating with large groups of people, as **Marla Falcon** does, It's a great job. Maria accompanies groups of holidaymakers on package tours. She knows she plays a central role in ensuring that people enjoy their holiday by providing them with practical support and information throughout the trip. 'It is important to allow people to do what they want, while at the same time making sure everybody is back on the minibus by the agreed time. And you must know the history of places you visit really well. Years back, I was embarrassed when a holidaymaker spotted some incorrect details in a commentary I was giving. Since then I've managed to attend regular local history classes to make sure it doesn't happen again.'

If the work of a tour guide seems a bit tame, **Patrick O'Connor** says that the job of adventure travel guide certainly offers excitement. Patrick leads trips to exotic locations around the globe, and he's quick to remind us that you need experience in a range of adventurous disciplines. 'People on these holidays are doing potentially dangerous activities, such as kayaking or diving. It's crucial to be able to exercise good judgment in difficult situations and be resourceful when dealing with the emergencies that are bound to arise. Once, I forgot to give somebody a life jacket and it could've been serious. This is a relatively new career, so educational institutions are only just beginning to offer programmes and qualifications.'

If you're thinking of becoming a travel agent, **Connie Ferguson** says you may want to give this career choice a little more thought. 'The job outlook isn't good right now because of the Internet. It's become much easier for people to make their own travel arrangements, though many people still need the advice of a travel professional.' Unlike other tourist jobs, you're based in an office, but you may get the opportunity to visit some destinations to evaluate the facilities on offer. Connie started by working as a reservations clerk in the travel agency, but the manager soon realised she had the skills to become a travel agent. 'Clients are well-informed and expect expert advice. I'm hoping to be able to start my own online travel business soon.'

Tourism offers something for everyone, with varying degrees of responsibilty. The nature of the job varies from working on a ski slope to developing marketing strategies to preparing gourmet meals. But for all tourism jobs you need to be adaptable, enjoy problem-solving and think on your feet.

Part 1

You **must** answer this question. Write your answer in **120–150** words in an appropriate style.

---

1   You and a friend have helped to organise a series of talks by guest speakers in the library. Your friend has sent you a letter with a small article from the local paper about last week's talk. Read the letter and the article. Then write to the newspaper editor using **all** the notes and asking him to publish another article.

Look at the article about last week's talk. Where did they get that information? Most of what they say is incorrect. Could you write a letter to the editor? I have no time to do it but I have made some notes.

The series of library talks have started on a disappointing note. The first talk had been announced for Tuesday, but was rescheduled for Friday at very short notice, without any explanation offered. The talk was about the protection of the environment, but the speaker had no new ideas to offer and the audience looked bored. The library should invite some younger speakers to contribute in future. Let's hope next week's talk will be more interesting.

speaker was ill, notice in library

Not true, an expert, and lots of questions!

age not important!

about African wildlife

Write your **letter**. You must use grammatically correct sentences with accurate spelling and punctuation in a style appropriate for the situation.

Part 2

Write an answer to **one** of the questions **2–4** in this part. Write an answer in **120–180** words in an appropriate style.

---

2   You have seen an advertisement for a part-time job.

> **Part-time waiters needed**
> for our new international restaurant.
>
> You need to:
> *   be good at working with people
> *   have some knowledge of foreign languages
> *   be willing to work flexible hours
>
> Write explaining why you would be suitable for the job to:
> Mr Roy Smith, manager of Carlton Restaurants.

Write your **letter of application**. Do not write any postal addresses.

3   You recently saw this notice in the local newspaper.

> **Can you write us a review of a TV soap opera you enjoy?**
>
> Tell us about the characters, what makes you keep on watching it and if you would recommend it to everyone.
>
> The best review wins a collection of DVDs!

Write your **review**.

4   Your teacher has asked you to write a story for an international magazine. The story must **begin** with the following words:

Maria looked at the map and realised she was completely lost. She decided to ask for help.

Write your **story**.

5   Answer **one** of the following two questions based on your reading of **one** of these set books.

(a) Author – *Name of book*
Character X in this book is sometimes misunderstood/treated unfairly by others. Write an **essay** saying when this happens and why, and explain how this character deals with those situations.

(b) Author – *Name of book*
The school wants to use this book in a literature workshop for teenagers. Write a **report** for the school, addressing the following points:
i)   Are the characters sufficiently interesting?
ii) Is the topic suitable for teenagers?
iii) Is the plot easy to follow?

For questions **1–12**, read the text below and decide which answer (**A**, **B**, **C** or **D**) best fits each gap. There is an example at the beginning (**0**).

In the exam you mark your answers on a separate answer sheet

Example:

0   A likes   **B** insists   **C** pretends   **D** stresses

The world's finest chocolates

Belgium **(0)** ...... to think of itself as the home of the finest chocolate in the world. If this **(1)** ...... is true, then the Place du Grand Sablon in Brussels must be the centre of the chocolate world. This square is not far from the city's Museum of Fine Arts and some of the country's **(2)** ...... chocolate shops can be found there, **(3)** ...... such internationally famous names as Wittamer, Godiva and Marcolini.

Marcolini is the most recent arrival in the square and is **(4)** ...... regarded as the most fashionable chocolate-maker in Belgium. The designers of the company's shop have evidently been **(5)** ...... up ideas from Emporio Armani a few doors down. The Marcolini shop has black walls, a white floor and staff who **(6)** ...... black and white shirts and resemble fashion models **(7)** ...... than salespeople.

As **(8)** ...... as the chocolates are concerned, these are displayed in impressive glass cases. Once you've **(9)** ...... your selection, you go over to the counter to pay, and get a wonderful close-up **(10)** ...... of a flowing fountain of melted chocolate.

Some Belgians would **(11)** ...... that the best examples of the country's skill at chocolate-making are the small chocolates called pralines. These have a hard outer shell of chocolate around a softer filling that **(12)** ...... in a variety of flavours. It was these that I decided to try.

0	**A**	likes	**B**	insists	**C**	pretends	**D**	stresses
1	**A**	accusation	**B**	claim	**C**	demand	**D**	challenge
2	**A**	leading	**B**	winning	**C**	ruling	**D**	beating
3	**A**	involving	**B**	enrolling	**C**	enclosing	**D**	including
4	**A**	wholly	**B**	greatly	**C**	widely	**D**	deeply
5	**A**	catching	**B**	picking	**C**	getting	**D**	copying
6	**A**	carry	**B**	wear	**C**	dress	**D**	clothe
7	**A**	instead	**B**	better	**C**	whereas	**D**	rather
8	**A**	soon	**B**	far	**C**	long	**D**	well
9	**A**	done	**B**	achieved	**C**	made	**D**	arrived
10	**A**	view	**B**	scene	**C**	sight	**D**	look
11	**A**	suggest	**B**	remind	**C**	persuade	**D**	inform
12	**A**	goes	**B**	offers	**C**	comes	**D**	gains

For questions **13–24**, read the text below and think of the word which best fits each gap. Use only **one** word in each gap. There is an example at the beginning **(0)**.

In the exam you write your answers IN CAPITAL LETTERS on a separate answer sheet.

Example: | 0 | W | I | T | H | | | | | | |

Health on holiday

Nobody wants to deal **(0)** ...... a medical emergency when they are on holiday. In practice you may not have **(13)** ...... choice in the matter, and it is best to be as **(14)** ...... prepared as possible. If you're travelling independently that means taking a medical kit.

The whole idea of the kit **(15)** ...... that you can carry it around with you, therefore it needs to be both light and compact. You can buy a pre-packed kit **(16)** ...... includes the main essential items, and this should be adequate in most situations. The problems that you are most likely to encounter will be minor inconveniences – cuts, stings, blisters, and so **(17)** ...... , and these can be sorted **(18)** ...... easily by using the things in the kit.

If you do decide to put your own kit together, however, do bear **(19)** ...... mind that it's pointless including items that you don't know **(20)** ...... to use; complicated bandages for example that only a trained nurse can put on correctly. It's much **(21)** ...... important to buy, read and preferably pack a good basic first aid book. This will help you to know **(22)** ...... to do in any less familiar situations as well as in any possible emergencies.

Finally, keep your first aid kit in a pocket or towards the top of your bag in **(23)** ...... you need to find it in **(24)** ...... hurry.

For questions **25–34**, read the text below. Use the word given in capitals at the end of some of the lines to form a word that fits the gap **in the same line**. There is an example at the beginning **(0)**.

In the exam you write your answers IN CAPITAL LETTERS on a separate answer sheet.

Example: | 0 | T | E | E | N | A | G | E | R | | | |

Music and maths

When I was a **(0)** ...... , I used to play the flute in my high   **TEEN**

school orchestra. **(25)** ...... , in much of the music that we   **FORTUNATELY**

played, the sound of the flute was needed only **(26)** ....   **OCCASION**

Therefore, I spent a lot of my time during the **(27)** ...... counting   **PERFORM**

the beats which the conductor indicated with each **(28)** ......   **MOVE**

of his baton.

Those minutes spent reciting 'one, two, three, four' under

my breath while the rest of the orchestra played seemed

(29) ...... to me. But they planted in my young brain the idea   **END**

that there must be a **(30)** ...... between music and numbers   **CONNECT**

and I decided to do a bit of research in the school library.

I soon learnt that history is full of **(31)** ...... to this idea, which   **REFER**

had been a source of **(32)** ...... for thinkers ever since the time   **FASCINATE**

of Pythagoras. Indeed, an early book on music by the Ancient

Roman philosopher Boethius is largely filled with diagrams and

explanations about the **(33)** ...... between music and mathematics.   **RELATION**

For me, out of the **(34)** ...... of orchestra practice, a new passion   **BORE**

was born.

Part 4

For questions **35–42**, complete the second sentence so that it has a similar meaning to the first sentence, using the word given. **Do not change the word given.** You must use between **two** and **five** words, including the word given. Here is an example **(0)**.

Example:

0 What type of music do you like best?

FAVOURITE

What .... type of music?

The space can be filled by the words 'is your favourite', so you write:

Example: | **0** | IS YOUR FAVOURITE |

In the exam you write only the missing words IN CAPITAL LETTERS on a separate answer sheet.

---

35 I had never been in that restaurant before.

FIRST

It .... I had ever been in that restaurant.

36 Luca was the only club member who hadn't paid his membership fees.

ALL

Apart .... the club members had paid their membership fees.

37 Simon doesn't object to his photograph appearing in the school brochure.

NO

Simon .... his photograph appearing in the magazine.

38 I find shopping on the Internet very boring.

GET

I find .... shopping on the Internet.

39 It is said that eating certain types of fish is very good for your health.

SUPPOSED

Eating certain types of fish ……………… very good for your health.

40 The hotel asks its guests if they prefer still or fizzy mineral water in their rooms.

RATHER

The hotel's guests are asked to say if ……………… have still or fizzy mineral water in their rooms.

41 During the carnival, they did not let people park in that part of the city.

ALLOWED

In that part of the city, parking ……………… the carnival was taking place.

42 Damian did not buy a ticket because the machine was not working properly.

IF

Damian would have bought a ticket ……………… working properly.

TEST 5: LISTENING

1 You hear the weather forecast on the radio.

What will the weather be like on Sunday?

A windier than on Saturday

B colder than on Saturday

C rainier than on Saturday

| | 1 |

2 You hear a character talking in a soap opera.

Who is he talking to?

A his boss

B his wife

C his trainer

| | 2 |

3 You hear an advertisement.

What is being advertised?

A a shop

B a publication

C a TV programme

| | 3 |

4 You hear part of a radio play.

How does the woman feel?

A nervous about something

B guilty about something

C bored by something

| | 4 |

5   You hear part of a programme on the subject of fashion.

What is the presenter's purpose?

A   to criticise certain attitudes

B   to complain about something

C   to recommend something to us

5

6   You overhear a woman talking about the flat she lives in.

Why is she thinking of selling it?

A   There's too little storage space.

B   She's disturbed by street noise.

C   It's a long way from her place of work.

6

7   You hear an announcement about a future wildlife event.

How will the event help the protection of wildlife?

A   by raising money

B   by informing the public

C   by recruiting volunteers

7

8   You overhear a family discussion about computer games.

Why does the young man like them?

A   They help him to relax after work.

B   They remind him of his childhood.

C   They make him more self-confident.

8

You will hear a radio programme about a bird called a peacock. For questions **9–18**, complete the sentences.

The peacock

People say that the peacock's tail looks similar to a

	9

The original home of the blue peacock is in

	10

Peacocks were first kept by people as long as

	11	years ago.

The peacock's | 12 | is long and thin.

The coloured spots on the peacock's tail are known as

	13

The female peahen is mostly | 14 | in colour.

In English, some people are described as being as

	15	as a peacock.

In the wild, peacocks usually live close to

	16	in the forest.

Peacocks usually spend time in trees when they want to

	17

At Peacock Paradise in Malaysia, you can see

	18	as well as birds.

Part 3

You will hear five different writers talking about their first novels. For questions **19–23**, choose from the list (**A–F**) what each writer says. Use the letters only once. There is one extra letter which you do not need to use.

A I learnt some of the skills of novel writing in a previous job.

Speaker 1 ⬜ **19**

B My earlier style of writing was not suitable for a novel.

Speaker 2 ⬜ **20**

C I was determined to write a novel that was true to life.

Speaker 3 ⬜ **21**

D I believe I should've been paid more to write this novel.

Speaker 4 ⬜ **22**

E This novel benefited from a course of study I attended.

Speaker 5 ⬜ **23**

F Being asked to write a novel came as a complete surprise to me.

Part 4

You will hear an interview with a man called David Shaw, who is a professional ceramicist, making pottery objects out of clay. For questions **24–30**, choose the best answer (**A**, **B** or **C**).

24 What does David say is an absolute requirement for people considering a career in ceramics?

    A They must feel a passion for it.
    B They must be physically very fit.   **24**
    C They must have enough patience.

25 David says it took him a long time to

    A develop his own style.
    B make his business profitable.   **25**
    C decide to work at ceramics full-time.

26 What does David find most enjoyable about his job?

    A the fact that the results are unpredictable
    B the feedback he gets from his customers   **26**
    C the knowledge that he creates useful pieces

27 What does David say he finds particularly difficult?

    A doing administrative tasks
    B finding time to research new ideas   **27**
    C finishing new commissions on time

28 What reason does David give for his recent success as a ceramicist?

    A He's been luckier than other ceramicists.
    B He's put in more effort than in the past.   **28**
    C He's started to follow certain fashions.

29 How does David feel about the possibility of teaching ceramics?

    A He feels unprepared for it.
    B He fears it might distract him.   **29**
    C He's unsure about finding time.

30 David advises people who want a career in ceramics to

    A talk to established ceramicists.
    B go to ceramics exhibitions.   **30**
    C attend a ceramics course.

Go to **www.iTests.com** for interactive exam practice.

Part 1 (3 minutes)

Answer these questions:

Tell us about the type of food you like to eat.

Do you prefer eating at home or eating out?

Who cooks most of the food you eat?

Do you prefer formal meals or informal snacks?

Part 2 (3 or 4 minutes)

Taking a break (compare, contrast and speculate)

Turn to pictures 1 and 2 on page 136, which show people taking a break.

Candidate A, compare and contrast these photographs, and say why the people may have needed the break. You have a minute to do this.

Candidate B, do you take breaks when you are studying?

Performers (compare, contrast and speculate)

Turn to pictures 1 and 2 on page 137, which show people performing in front of an audience.

Candidate B, compare and contrast these photographs, and say how the performers and the audience may be feeling. You have a minute to do this.

Candidate A, do you like the circus?

Part 3 (3 or 4 minutes)

The best way to learn languages (discuss and evaluate)

Turn to the pictures on page 138, which show different ways of learning languages. Imagine that you are giving advice to a person who has never learnt a foreign language before.

Talk about how effective these different ways of leaning might be and decide what advice you would give.

Part 4 (3 or 4 minutes)

Answer these questions:

What is your favourite way of learning?

Do you think that learning languages is different from learning other subjects? Why/Why not?

Do you feel you would be able to teach your own language to a friend? How difficult would that be?

TEST 6:
READING

Part 1

You are going to read an article about celebrity assistants. For questions **1–8**, choose the answer (**A**, **B**, **C** or **D**) which you think fits best according to the text.

ASSISTANTS TO THE STARS

It stands to reason that a city like Los Angeles, which is home to so many of the famous and the semi-famous, would have an Association of Celebrity Personal Assistants (ACPA). The organisation describes personal assistants as 'multitasking', as 'possessing the most resourceful, creative, insightful, and results-driven abilities.'

When I first got in touch with Josef Csongei, the organisation's president, he was initially reluctant to talk to me because I was a journalist. As he sees it, celebrity personal assistants have not always been treated fairly by the press. But despite this, and all the hard work and lack of appreciation that can come with this line of work, he explained, the jobs were still widely sought after. He noted that people regularly travelled great distances to attend a seminar titled 'Becoming a Celebrity

21 Personal Assistant', run by the ACPA. To prove his point, he told me about Dean Johnson. In the coming weeks, I heard this story from a number of assistants, including Johnson himself, and every time it left me baffled.

The story begins one night in September 1994, with Dean Johnson sitting at home in Columbia, South Carolina. Johnson is a single, 32-year-old business executive in charge of marketing and advertising at a sizeable company in the healthcare industry. It is 11 pm and he's looking to unwind in front of the television after a long day's work. A repeat of a talk show appears on the screen, and the host introduces her four guests: the celebrity personal assistants for Whoopi Goldberg, Roseanne Barr, Burt Reynolds and Carol Burnett. As these assistants talk about flying on private jets and attending Hollywood parties, Johnson reaches for a pen and starts taking notes. Without wasting another minute, he picks up the phone, calls directory enquiries in Los Angeles, and asks for the home phone numbers of the four assistants on the show.

Only one of them is listed: Ron Holder, who works for Whoopi Goldberg. Johnson dials his number, and a minute later Holder picks up the phone. 'He said I was very lucky to get through,' Johnson told me. 'Apparently, in the three months since he had appeared on that talk show, he had received about 200 phone calls from people like me. He was in the process of disconnecting his phone, but he was nice enough to chat with me for a while.' During their conversation, Holder told Johnson that he should consider attending the 'Becoming a Celebrity Personal Assistant' seminar in Los Angeles.

For someone like Johnson, with almost no connections in the industry, the notion of moving out to Los Angeles to become a celebrity personal assistant, something he did two months later, was extremely courageous – there's no denying that. The typical American story of the guy in the remote provinces who falls in love with the glamour of the silver screen, packs up all his possessions and moves out to Hollywood to become a star is almost a century old. But Johnson's story offered a new twist: he moved out to Hollywood to become an assistant to a star.

Of the thousands of people who work in Holly-wood: agents, lawyers, stylists, publicists, business managers and others, many hope to rub shoulders with the biggest stars. What's unique about celebrity personal assistants is that such proximity

77 appears to be the only perk their profession offers. Most describe the bulk of their work as drudgery: doing laundry, fetching groceries, paying bills. Assistants typically make about $56,000 a year – hardly a fortune by Hollywood standards, especially given the round-the-clock obligations they often have. What's more, the job is rarely a stepping stone to fame: celebrity personal assistants are, on average, aged about 38, right in the middle of their professional lives, and most of the ones I met described their line of work as a lifelong profession. For them, being an assistant was not the means to an end but an end in itself.

1   When the writer first contacted him, Josef Csongei was

    A   angry about something she had written.
    B   suspicious of her because of her profession.
    C   surprised that she was interested in his organisation.
    D   pleased that she recognised the importance of assistants.

2   The phrase 'to prove his point' (line 21) refers to Csongei's belief that celebrity
    assistants

    A   enjoy travelling as part of the job.
    B   are not given the appreciation they deserve.
    C   do a job that many other people would like to do.
    D   need to do a course before they start looking for work.

3   At the beginning of the story about Dean Johnson, we learn that

    A   he had turned on the television in order to relax.
    B   he was dissatisfied with the work he was doing.
    C   he had always wanted to work in the film industry.
    D   he often watched television programmes about celebrities.

4   What was Dean's immediate reaction to what he saw on the programme?

    A   He wrote down the contact details of the four interviewees.
    B   He decided which of the four interviewees he wanted to talk to.
    C   He started making enquiries about how to find the people on the show.
    D   He read through his notes carefully before getting in touch with anyone.

5   How did Ron Holder respond to Dean's phone call?

    A   He refused to enter into a long conversation with Dean.
    B   He was angry that anyone had been able to get his number.
    C   He complained about being disturbed on his home number.
    D   He was willing to give Dean some advice and information.

6   In the fifth paragraph, the writer suggests that Dean Johnson

    A   never achieved his aim of becoming a personal assistant.
    B   was brave to go and look for a new career in Los Angeles.
    C   really wanted to become a star rather than a personal assistant.
    D   lived to regret his decision to give up everything in his old life.

7   What does the word 'perk' (line 77) mean?

    A   extra work required by a job
    B   something unexpected in a job
    C   a benefit of doing a particular job
    D   an unpleasant job that has to be done

8   In the final paragraph, we learn that celebrity assistants

    A   tend to see the job as their career goal.
    B   are relatively well paid for what they do.
    C   find the job gets too demanding as they get older.
    D   often move into other aspects of the film industry.

You are going to read a magazine article about two islands. Seven sentences have been removed from the article. Choose from the sentences **A–H** the one which fits each gap (**9–15**). There is one extra sentence which you do not need to use.

Cayman Brac and Little Cayman

Few destinations feel further from life in the twenty-first century than Cayman Brac and Little Cayman – the less well-known sister islands of Grand Cayman in the Caribbean. A stay on one – or both – is the perfect tonic for anyone who is tired, stressed and in need of a proper break.

It's not all about relaxing in the sun, though, and lovers of the outdoors will be in their element. **9** The Cayman Islands form one of the world's top three dive destinations and divers flock from all corners of the world to explore their waters.

The range of marine life is so phenomenal that a large part of the *The Blue Planet* television series was filmed here. Those seeking a once-in-a-lifetime underwater experience can stop in the Cayman Islands and book a trip in a submarine that takes them down 300 metres to discover weird and wonderful creatures rarely seen nearer the surface. **10**

Although Cayman Brac and Little Cayman have fundamental similarities, they are quite different in geography and atmosphere. Little Cayman is not really built up apart from a few small hotels, a couple of very good local restaurants and a quirky museum. **11**

It goes without saying that the diving around Little Cayman is excellent. An extra draw is the coral reef called the Bloody Bay Wall. **12** Here, amid the wall's colourful coral, divers will find butterfly fish, angelfish and bonefish. If they are lucky, a turtle or two will swim lazily past. Even if you don't dive, there is so much to see just below the surface that snorkelling is fascinating enough.

But Little Cayman is not just about the sea. **13** Its wonderfully varied natural environment is best seen by exploring the island by bike. All in all, Little Cayman has a unique appeal. Who could fail to be charmed by an island where the fire engine is bigger than the airport building, and where iguanas have right of way on the road?

Cayman Brac, although not much bigger, is quite different. **14** The locals are friendly people who love to chat, each one with their own fascinating story to tell.

The landscape in Cayman Brac is also surprisingly hilly, with dense woodland, secret caves and a vertical cliff that rises fifty metres on the east side of the island.

This diverse scenery has created a unique natural habitat that can be explored by walking the eight miles of public footpaths and hiking trails. Cayman Brac is a natural stopping-off point for migrating birds. **15** Great fishing opportunities and a selection of excellent hotels complete the picture.

Whether you want to explore the underwater world or keep your head above water, a holiday on either Cayman Brac or Little Cayman is guaranteed to leave you feeling as good as new. These laid-back islands will capture your imagination like few other places on earth ever could.

A It starts at 7 metres deep and suddenly plunges to a staggering 2000 metres.

B As well as these visitors, it is also home to nearly 200 resident species, including an endangered parrot.

C This should not be a problem as there are now at least two airlines which fly to the islands regularly.

D Back on land, there is more nature to be discovered.

E They will love the walking and the cycling, and in particular the wonderful opportunities for diving and snorkelling.

F It is this lack of development that attracts visitors to its shores year after year.

G With roughly 1600 inhabitants to its neighbour's 120, it is much livelier.

H More people have travelled in space than have been down this far into the depths of the sea.

Part 3

You are going to read a magazine article about bookshop managers. For questions
16–30, choose from the people (**A–D**). The people may be chosen more than once.

A	Mandy Stocks
B	Andrew Welson
C	Jane Harvard
D	James Darry

Which bookshop manager

mentions a way of adapting to survive in the age of the Internet?	16
believes the shop has another function apart from the selling of books?	17
is unsure about the amount of money the bookshop makes?	18
believes customers are attracted by the way the books are displayed?	19
changed their mind about the chosen location of the bookshop?	20
is prepared to reduce the price of some books?	21
is doubtful about being able to obtain the funds needed to expand?	22
spent some time finding out information before opening the shop?	23
is critical of the customer service offered by some bookshops?	24
explains why a previous job was given up?	25
is proud of the shop's stock of books for the very young?	26
mentions a link between customers' occupations and their choice of books?	27
has some knowledge about the contents of all the books on sale?	28
is able to organise cultural events on the premises?	29
mentions the fact that local people prefer the shop to larger ones?	30

The bestsellers

Do you buy books on the internet or in bookshops?
Dan Branson *visits four successful bookshop managers …*

Mandy Stocks: Saville Books   This shop is small and beautiful and it does not stock bestsellers, preferring to promote less well-known young authors. The children's section demonstrates the difference in philosophy between this and most other shops. 'We carry a vast range of books that reflect reality,' says Mandy. 'The vast majority of bookshops don't show children the world the way it is.' You could question the need to have CDs, tapes and so many other products in a bookshop, but Mandy says her bookshop would be incomplete without them. 'This shop is also an information centre,' she says. There are some much bigger bookshops in the area, but Mandy says buyers from the area are loyal and realise that her shop offers them a better service. Earlier this month, *Saville Books* was named Bookseller of the Year in recognition of the effort and imagination that Mandy has put into the shop. Mandy would like to enlarge the shop. 'It'll be hard to find somebody willing to invest money in it,' she says.

Andrew Welson: Lonestar Bookshop
Andrew is a very experienced bookseller. He ran a second-hand bookshop for several years until the need to increase his income made him apply for a position as manager of *Lonestar*. 'There is a huge disparity in quality among large bookshops,' he says. 'The best are very good, but others aren't, because the people who are at the face of helping the customer don't feel they are valued and the managers tend not to have a history of bookselling. You need to be passionate about the things you are selling.' The shop is modern and stylish. 'We only have a certain amount of space and what we are trying to do is stock the kind of books that our customers – mostly university students and young professionals – come to this shop for. But I also stock the popular books everyone's talking about, like *The Da Vinci Code*, for example.' Andrew gives a lot of attention to making his shop window eye-catching and interesting. 'It is incredibly important,' he says.

Jane Harvard: Brunswick Bookshop   Jane opened the *Brunswick Bookshop* last November, and it's the sort of place that captivates you as you go through the door. She says she is doing 'fantastically', though she admits she does not know how fantastically because her accountant has not finished calculating her profits. Jane has been in bookselling at three different shops, for fifteen years, and last year she decided to take the plunge and set up on her own. She was planning to open a shop in a fashionable part of the city, but then discovered a less well-off market area. 'The moment I saw it I knew it was right because it's a community street. I came and sat in the cafés and listened to conversations to see what kind of people lived here. They were well educated but didn't necessarily have much money.' Everything in her shop Jane wants to read herself. 'Obviously you don't have time to read them all, but I've got a pretty good idea of what's in most of them,' she says.

James Darry: Darry Books   *Darry Books* is light, airy, modern and welcoming. It's got a strong children's section, a coffee bar, and also a space upstairs for author talks and presentations of new books. James is a former school head and left his job to start the bookshop. Why did he do it? 'I was having a conversation with a colleague one day, about what we could have done instead of teaching, and I said I would have had a bookshop. I realised I wanted a change. A year later I opened this shop, but it hasn't been easy. The competition from larger chains of bookshops is horrendous, so I offer lots of discounts, but not on a good-quality book that might be bought as a gift.' James has four full-time employees. 'We treat bookselling as a proper career and the staff are motivated, interested and well paid. Nowadays, you can buy any book on websites, the book trade is changing fast and we have to change with it, by offering customers that special personal touch.

You **must** answer this question. Write your answer in **120–150** words in an appropriate style.

1 You have printed off this advertisement from the internet about adventure activity holidays. Read the advertisement and the notes you have made. Then write an email to the organisers, using **all** your notes.

DO YOU THINK HOLIDAYS HAVE BECOME DULL AND BORING?

ARE YOU LOOKING FOR SOMETHING EXCITING AND FUN? — *yes!*

THEN YOU HAVE COME TO THE RIGHT PLACE!

Never done it, lessons? — CANOEING, SKYDIVING, WHITEWATER RAFTING AND MUCH MORE!

SIMPLY CONTACT US AND WE WILL DESIGN A TAILOR-MADE ACTIVITY HOLIDAY FOR YOU. DON'T FORGET TO TELL US HOW FIT YOU ARE, AND WHAT SPORT YOU PRACTISE REGULARLY. — *one week, water sports, nothing too dangerous!*

travel insurance? — ALL OUR PRICES INCLUDE TRAVEL, ACCOMMODATION AND MEALS.

WE LOOK FORWARD TO SEEING YOU ON ONE OF OUR ACTIVITY HOLIDAYS VERY SOON!

Write your **email**. You must use grammatically correct sentences with accurate spelling and punctuation in a style appropriate for the situation.

Part 2

Write an answer to **one** of the questions **2–4** in this part. Write an answer in **120–180** words in an appropriate style.

2   You have had a class discussion about downloading music from the Internet. Now your teacher has asked you to write an essay, giving your views on the following statement:

Soon everybody will be downloading music from the Internet and music shops will disappear.

Write your **essay**.

3   You recently saw this notice in the local newspaper.

> Write a review of a TV nature programme and win a camera!
>
> Include information about the content of the programme and the locations it shows and say if you think it is for all ages.

Write your **review**.

4   The school library has decided to buy new books, magazines and DVDs for its Teenage Section. You have been asked to write a report to the principal, saying what kind of materials would be most popular with teenagers and why. You should also say whether the materials should be for loan or only to be used in the library.

Write your **report**.

5   Answer **one** of the following two questions based on your reading of **one** of these set books.

(a) Author – *Name of book*

I have just finished reading this book and I think some of the characters are very unrealistic. Nobody would act like that in the real world. What do you think? Emma

Write a **letter** to Emma saying whether you agree with her or not, and giving examples and reasons for your opinions.

(b) Author – *Name of book*
In this novel, there are two characters that do not get on well together. Write an **essay** describing some of the conflicts between them and say whether their relationship changes at the end.

Part 1

For questions **1–12**, read the text below and decide which answer (**A**, **B**, **C** or **D**) best fits each gap. There is an example at the beginning **(0)**.

In the exam you mark your answers on a separate answer sheet.

Example:

0 **A** got   **B** found   **C** reached   **D** received

My first expedition

When I was about twelve, I **(0)** …… the chance to go to western China, looking for rare plants in an extraordinary area of mountains and forests. I wasn't all that **(1)** …… in plants, but my dad's a botanist by **(2)** …… and he was going as assistant to Professor Beall, who was leading the expedition.

It was an important international expedition and my name was **(3)** …… not on the list of participants. But at the **(4)** …… moment, one of the experts broke his ankle and so had to **(5)** …… out. It was impossible to get anyone else to go at such **(6)** …… notice, so my dad suggested taking me, for the experience.

I think the professor was so surprised that he agreed without thinking, but he obviously began to **(7)** …… doubts as soon as the plane was in the air. I remember him **(8)** …… that he hoped I wasn't going to run around and **(9)** …… on rare specimens! As if I was a little kid.

My dad didn't say anything as bad as that, but he did say that he hoped he wasn't going to **(10)** …… bringing me. I tried to be really quiet so they would forget I was there. They didn't realise it at the **(11)** …… , but my ambition was to get a photo of a wild panda. And, of course, in the end that's **(12)** …… what I did.

0	**A**	got	**B**	found	**C**	reached	**D**	received
1	**A**	fascinated	**B**	keen	**C**	interested	**D**	fond
2	**A**	work	**B**	profession	**C**	job	**D**	employment
3	**A**	completely	**B**	definitely	**C**	particularly	**D**	confidently
4	**A**	late	**B**	final	**C**	last	**D**	end
5	**A**	drop	**B**	slip	**C**	fall	**D**	step
6	**A**	quick	**B**	brief	**C**	fast	**D**	short
7	**A**	have	**B**	see	**C**	do	**D**	feel
8	**A**	speaking	**B**	telling	**C**	talking	**D**	saying
9	**A**	tread	**B**	spoil	**C**	squash	**D**	ruin
10	**A**	discourage	**B**	regret	**C**	disappoint	**D**	apologise
11	**A**	minute	**B**	point	**C**	event	**D**	time
12	**A**	perfectly	**B**	correctly	**C**	exactly	**D**	accurately

For questions **13–24**, read the text below and think of the word which best fits each gap. Use only one word in each gap. There is an example at the beginning **(0)**.

In the exam you write your answers IN CAPITAL LETTERS on a separate answer sheet.

Example: | 0 | U | P | | | | | | | | | |

Shopping trolley joins the push for fitness

Although some shoppers may already find supermarket trolleys quite hard to push **(0)** ...... and down the aisles, one supermarket chain is about to make the task even harder. Next week sees the introduction of the **(13)** ...... called Trim Trolley, **(14)** ...... is designed to transform the typical forty-minute supermarket visit **(15)** ...... a gentle workout.

The Trim Trolley can be set at different levels of resistance, making it harder or easier to push. It is also able to measure both the customer's heart rate **(16)** ...... the number of calories burnt through sensors on the handle. Shoppers **(17)** ...... thought to burn about 160 calories during a typical forty-minute visit to the supermarket. Pushing the Trim Trolley for that length of time **(18)** ...... the resistance level at seven, the average person would burn as **(19)** ...... as 280 calories. In **(20)** ...... words, the equivalent of a twenty-minute swim. At the highest resistance level, a shopping trip could replace a trip to the gym.

As well as pointing **(21)** ...... to people that shopping is a subconscious form of exercise, the designers also hope to encourage shoppers to **(22)** ...... more attention to their health generally. A spokesperson for the supermarket said: 'We hope it will make people more aware of **(23)** ...... they are putting in their trolleys. The chocolate cakes may be easier to resist **(24)** ...... you've got calorie levels on your mind!'

Part 3

For questions **25–34**, read the text below. Use the word given in capitals at the end of some of the lines to form a word that fits the gap **in the same line**. There is an example at the beginning **(0)**.

In the exam you write your answers IN CAPITAL LETTERS on a separate answer sheet.

Example:

| 0 | T | W | E | N | T | I | E | T | H | | |

Toy story

In the second half of the **(0)** ...... century, toys like model   **TWENTY**

cars and Barbie dolls made the perfect gift for young children.

Most of these toys were played with until they fell apart, but

others were looked after very **(25)** ...... by children who were   **CAREFUL**

more interested in building a **(26)** .... Today most of these   **COLLECT**

toys belong to adults and some have become valuable antiques.

Barbie has been popular with girls since she made her first

(27) ...... in toy shops over fifty years ago. She has been   **APPEAR**

sold in hundreds of different fashionable **(28)** ...... as well as the   **FIT**

clothes suitable for a **(29)** ...... of professions including secretary,   **VARY**

flight attendant and astronaut. Today **(30)** ...... clothed Barbies   **FULL**

are sold for hundreds of dollars, the most expensive being

those in **(31)** ...... condition, with their original packaging   **DAMAGED**

and accessories.

If you're interested in starting a toy collection, another good

(32) ...... are Japanese battery-operated robots of the 1960s.   **INVEST**

Although not very **(33)** ...... by today's standards, some of   **IMPRESS**

these toys are now very rare. If they are in full **(34)** ...... order,   **WORK**

they can cost thousands of dollars.

Part 4

For questions **35–42**, complete the second sentence so that it has a similar meaning to the first sentence, using the word given. **Do not change the word given.** You must use between **two** and **five** words, including the word given. Here is an example **(0)**.

Example:

0   What type of music do you like best?

FAVOURITE

What .... type of music?

The space can be filled by the words 'is your favourite', so you write:

Example: | 0 | | IS YOUR FAVOURITE |

In the exam you write only the missing words IN CAPITAL LETTERS on a separate answer sheet.

---

35   Pete hadn't expected to see so many old friends at the party.

SURPRISE

It came .... to see so many old friends at the party.

36   Although she was a good runner, Wendy never succeeded in winning an Olympic medal.

MANAGED

Although she was a good runner, Wendy .... an Olympic medal.

37   Jacqui and I were sitting by ourselves at the back of the coach.

OWN

Jacqui and I were sitting .... at the back of the coach.

38   The country's economic problems are less serious than people had been led to believe.

AS

The country's economic problems .... people had been led to believe.

39 Adam hadn't finished his homework when Remy arrived.

STILL

Adam .... his homework, when Remy arrived.

40 I think you should complain to your boss.

WERE

If I .... a complaint to my boss.

41 For me, the film was spoilt by the awful soundtrack.

MY

In .... the awful soundtrack which spoilt the film.

42 Toronto has been my home since last March.

LIVING

I have .... last March.

Part 1

You will hear people talking in eight different situations. For questions **1–8**, choose the best answer (**A**, **B** or **C**).

1   You hear part of a talk by a man who works for a tourist company.

     What is his role in the company?

     A   He trains the guides.

     B   He chooses the destinations.

     C   He designs the advertisements.

     | 1 |

2   You overhear two people talking about a film.

     Why didn't the man enjoy it?

     A   He was distracted by noise.

     B   His seat was uncomfortable.

     C   The sound volume was too low.

     | 2 |

3   You hear a woman talking about running in a marathon.

     Why did she decide to run?

     A   She knew it would be good for her level of fitness.

     B   She'd been wanting to do it since her schooldays.

     C   She was too embarrassed to refuse to do it.

     | 3 |

4   On the radio, you hear a man talking about an antique calculator.

     What does he say about it?

     A   It's just been stolen.

     B   It's just been found.

     C   It's just been sold.

     | 4 |

5   You hear a politician talking about facilities for the young in her area.

In her opinion, what is needed?

A   a library

B   a leisure centre

C   an Internet café

5

6   You overhear a woman talking about a full-time job in a theatre.

Why did she decide not to apply for it?

A   She was used to working part-time.

B   She would have had to work evenings.

C   She felt she lacked the right qualifications.

6

7   You hear part of an interview with a comedian who organises what he calls 'laughter workshops'.

What does he want to teach the participants?

A   how to make friends more easily

B   how to become more self-confident

C   how to help others overcome problems

7

8   You hear a woman talking about learning to fly a plane.

How did she feel during her first lesson?

A   alarmed by the way the plane moved

B   relieved that it seemed relatively easy

C   confused by the instructor's comments

8

Part 2

You will hear an interview with a man called Daren Howarth, who works as a carbon coach. For questions **9–18**, complete the sentences.

The carbon coach

Daren says that a carbon coach works full-time as a

[_____ **9**] with various clients.

Before becoming a carbon coach, Daren trained to be an

[_____ **10**]

When assessing a family's carbon footprint, Daren looks first at their

[_____ **11**]

Daren uses what's called a [_____ **12**]

to see how much electricity things use.

Daren points out that [_____ **13**]

will help pay for roof insulation.

Daren feels that using [_____ **14**] of the old type is

the worst waste of energy he sees.

Daren helped to reduce a band's carbon footprint at

[_____ **15**] as well as on its CDs.

Daren mentions a new type of green home called an

[_____ **16**]

The new green home uses both the sun and

[_____ **17**] to produce electricity.

Daren suggests buying a [_____ **18**] which gives

more information about the new green home.

Part 3

You will hear five different people talking about the sport of hill walking. For questions **19–23**, choose from the list (**A–F**) the reason why each person took up the sport. Use the letters only once. There is one extra letter which you do not need to use.

A Other sports had failed to improve my fitness.

Speaker 1 | 19 |

B I had plans to do some serious climbing later on.

Speaker 2 | 20 |

C My ambition was to lead hill-walking groups.

Speaker 3 | 21 |

D I was hoping it would solve a health problem I had.

Speaker 4 | 22 |

E I wanted to be able to enjoy hill walking with other people.

Speaker 5 | 23 |

F I realised it would be more fun than other sporting activities.

Part 4

You will hear an interview with a woman called Jennie Thorpe, who is a trapeze artist in a circus. For questions **24–30**, choose the best answer (**A**, **B** or **C**).

24 Jennie got her present job when her manager saw her performing at

   A a gymnastics competition.
   B a circus school.
   C a ballet show.

24

25 Why does Jennie feel a need to practise just after the end of a show?

   A She is able to do more difficult things then.
   B She is too tense to be able to relax immediately.
   C She is able to sleep better afterwards.

25

26 What does Jennie say about earning a living as a trapeze artist?

   A It's hard if you have no contract.
   B It's unlikely after a certain age.
   C It's difficult for most performers.

26

27 According to Jennie, what distinguishes great trapeze artists from the rest?

   A They have the lightest bodies.
   B They perform without a safety net.
   C They have an abililty to keep calm.

27

28 What does Jennie find the most difficult thing to get used to?

   A having to get up early every day
   B damaging her hands on the trapeze
   C feeling pain in her muscles

28

29 In Jennie's opinion, circus skills have helped some school students by

   A making them physically stronger.
   B increasing their ability to study.
   C improving their social interaction.

29

30 What does Jennie want to do next?

   A do a training course
   B get a teaching job
   C open a circus school

30

Go to **www.iTests.com** for interactive exam practice.

Part 1 (3 minutes)

Answer these questions:

What type of things do you like to read?

Do you prefer to read a novel or see the film? Why?

Which film actor or actress do you like most? Why?

Part 2 (3 or 4 minutes)

Communicating (compare, contrast and speculate)

Turn to pictures 1 and 2 on page 139, which show people communicating in different ways.

Candidate A, compare and contrast these photographs, and say how necessary it may be for the people to communicate in these ways. You have a minute to do this.

Candidate B, do you use the telephone a lot?

Competitions (compare, contrast and speculate)

Turn to pictures 1 and 2 on page 140, which show people taking part in competitions.

Candidate B, compare and contrast these photographs, and say how the people may be feeling. You have a minute to do this.

Candidate A, do you like competitions?

Part 3 (3 or 4 minutes)

Interesting jobs (discuss and evaluate)

Turn to the pictures on page 141, which show people doing five different jobs. Imagine that your college has invited these people to talk to students about what they like and don't like about their jobs.

Talk about how difficult or easy it might be to do these jobs and decide what questions you would want to ask the five guest speakers.

Part 4 (3 or 4 minutes)

Answer these questions:

What would be your ideal job?

When you get a job, would you like to work part-time or full-time? Why?

How would you feel if you had to work at weekends?

Why have the people chosen these places to study?

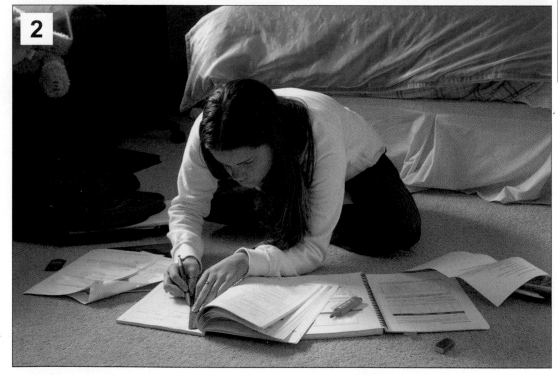

Useful phrases

Well, the people in these photos are studying in *very different places. In the first photo*, there are several students in a library, *in the second*, a girl is studying in her bedroom.

The students seem to be working in pairs, helping each other. I think studying with other people is enjoyable – you can share information and learn more easily. *Perhaps* they have chosen to study in the library because they can have easy access to lots of books.

I get the impression that the girl is not very comfortable sitting on the floor. *She looks like she's* a bit anxious. She's clearly concentrating hard on her work. *She may have chosen* to work in her bedroom because she can be sure she won't be interrupted.

How good are these forms of exercise for the people in the photos?

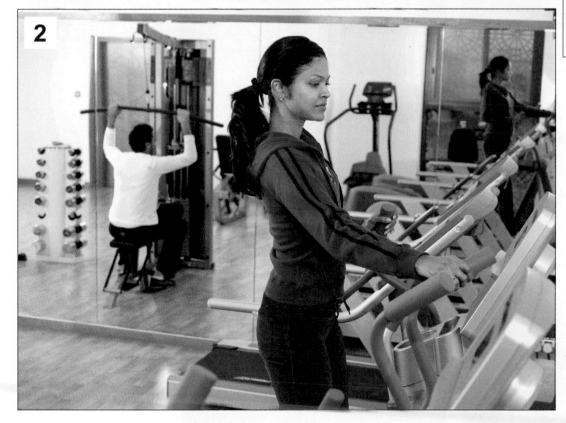

Useful phrases

The people in these photos are doing very different types of exercise. The boys in the first photo are playing football and *they seem to be enjoying themselves more than* the people in the second photograph, who are exercising in a gym. For children, I think outdoor sport is healthier than working out in a gym. Football is an excellent form of exercise and it also teaches children the importance of teamwork.

In the second photo, *I think the young woman looks bored. She probably exercises* several times a week to keep fit or to avoid putting on weight. The man at the back is doing weightlifting. *Perhaps they both have* full-time jobs and they come to the gym after work.

- How serious are these problems for the people involved?
- What can people do to avoid these problems?

Useful phrases

Some of these problems are really serious, *don't you think*?

In my opinion, some of these situations can be frightening if you are travelling on your own in a foreign country. For example, getting ill and needing to see a doctor … *Would you agree with that?*

Yes, absolutely. That's much more serious than having a long delay at the airport … *What do you think?*

I'm not sure I agree with that. Having to wait for hours can be really upsetting, particularly for people with children … *What do you think of the man who is stuck in a traffic queue? Is that a serious problem?*

Do you think some of these problems can be avoided?

Well, the man who has lost his way could have planned his journey better, *don't you think?*

What type of person would choose these holidays?

How do you think the people might be feeling?

- How difficult or easy might it be to do these jobs?
- Which would be the most popular with students?

How do you think the people and the animals are feeling?

TEST 3, PAPER 5: SPEAKING

How much may the people be enjoying these experiences?

- Which pictures would you choose to talk about and why?
- Which picture would you choose for a poster about your talk?

Why do you think the people may have chosen these forms of transport?

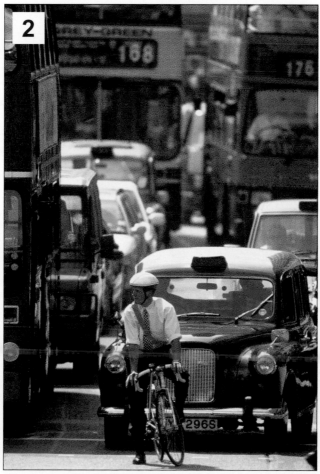

How interesting do you think these games are for different age groups?

- In which areas would the visitors need advice from you?
- In which areas do you think your advice is not so necessary?

Why do you think the people may have needed a break?

How do you think the audience and the performers may be feeling?

- How effective are these different ways of learning?
- What advice would you give?

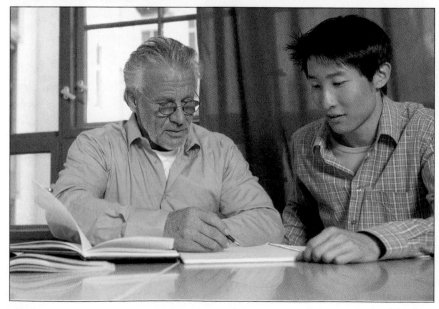

How necessary do you think it is for the people to communicate in these ways?

How do you think these people are feeling?

1

2

- How easy or difficult might it be to do these jobs?
- What questions would you want to ask the guest speakers?

Answer Key

Test 1, Paper 1: Reading (page 4)

Part 1: Driving in the desert

1 A: Incorrect: She drove there, but it's not why she went.
   B: Incorrect: She did drive in the desert there, but that's not why she went.
   C: Incorrect: She doesn't say that any of her family lived there.
   D: Correct: She wanted to prove she could adapt to new situations.
2 A: Incorrect: This is not the main consideration.
   B: Incorrect: This is not what she says.
   C: Incorrect: Everything she says suggests the race is very serious.
   D: Correct: 'same goal and the same way of working'.
3 A: Incorrect: Not what 'this' refers to.
   B: Incorrect: Not what 'this' refers to.
   C: Correct: 'this' refers to the previous sentence.
   D: Incorrect: Not what 'this' refers to.
4 A: Incorrect: This wasn't her 'greatest fear'.
   B: Correct: 'the thing that scared us most'.
   C: Incorrect: It was the ground that got damaged, not the car.
   D: Incorrect: It was the organisers who would rescue her.
5 A: Incorrect: Participating in the rally cost more.
   B: Incorrect: She had to hire it.
   C: Correct: 'It's always the people you least expect who help you most.'
   D: Incorrect: She had no breakdown.
6 A: Incorrect: We don't know what they thought of her driving skills.
   B: Correct: The word 'jaunt' suggests something not very serious.
   C: Incorrect: We don't know whether they thought this.
   D: Incorrect: It's implied that they might have sponsored men's rallying.
7 A: Correct: 'they're less good at anticipating problems'.
   B: Incorrect: She doesn't link the two things.
   C: Incorrect: This is not what she thinks.
   D: Incorrect: She doesn't mention this.
8 A: Correct: 'it's also a big thing on my CV'.
   B: Incorrect: We don't know what they think, only how she feels.
   C: Incorrect: She says 'next year' not every year.
   D: Incorrect: No, it helps her deal with her problems.

Part 2: Music to get fit by

9 H: Link between 'close companions' and 'the link between'. Link between 'Dr Costas …' and 'He'.
10 G: Link between 'synchronisation of …' and 'the right music'. Link between 'increased' and 'up'.
11 A: Link between 'disassociation' and 'this word'.
12 C: Link between 'rules' and 'One of them'. Link between 'music must be' and 'music should mirror'.
13 F: Link between 'friend' and 'he'. Link between 'mistake' and 'cooling down to …'
14 D: Link between 'songs' and 'limited number of them'. Link between 'complaint' and 'This is mostly because …'.
15 B: Link between 'diverse range of sports' and 'for example, golfers …'

Part 3: Why do people start writing blogs?

16 D: 'a useful tool in my future job …'
17 A: 'my blog is a business tool.'
18 C: 'So it's not the thing to do if …'
19 E: 'had serious spelling problems …'
20 B: 'I needed to get some good content …'
21 C: 'if I make mistakes I learn from …'
22 A: 'I felt confident that I already knew …'
23 E: 'my writing was getting better'
24 B: 'I was basically a nobody …'
25 B: 'It was amazing!'
26 E: 'incredibly, I got noticed by employers.'
27 D: 'Writing a 750-word article is …'
28 C: 'refreshing to be able to step outside …'
29 A: 'they kept them hidden under their beds.'
30 D: 'since then I've helped others launch …'

The total score is adjusted to give a mark out of 20.

Test 1, Paper 2: Writing (page 10)

Part 1

Question 1
Style: informal
Content: 1 Say why you cannot join her.
         2 Give information about gyms.
         3 Explain what she must do if she goes just twice a week.
         4 Offer to help and suggest a time and place.

Part 2

Question 2
Style: neutral or semi-formal
Content: Describe your friend, the activities you did together, and explain why you got on well.

Question 3
Style: Formal or neutral. Avoid informal expressions. Use clear paragraphs.
Content: 1 Describe some of the things exhibited.
         2 Say whether the information was enough / well presented, etc.
         3 Mentions the facilities (e.g. seating areas, café) and say what they were like.

4 Say whether other students should be encouraged to go.

Question 4
Style: Semi-formal or neutral. Use clear paragraphs.
Content: 1 Say what Roy saw and why it showed something was wrong.
2 Say what Roy did after that.
3 Explain how it all ends.

Question 5(a)
Style: formal
Content: Mention any changes in appearance, character, opinions or behaviour, and explain how these were the result of certain events in the plot.

Question 5(b)
Style: informal or neutral
Content: Say why it is worth / not worth reading. Make sure the reasons you give refer specifically to parts of the book.

The total score is adjusted to give a mark out of 20.

Test 1, Paper 3: Use of English
(page 12)

Part 1: Don't forget your hat
1 B: 'out and about' is a fixed phrase.
2 A: 'do the job' is a common expression.
3 B: 'sending out' matches the meaning of 'lost' in the next sentence.
4 D: the other words do not give the idea of quantity.
5 C: the other words cannot followed by the preposition 'on'.
6 D: the other words do not collocate with 'warm'.
7 C: the other words are not usually used to talk about sunlight.
8 A: the other three words would need a new subject.
9 D: the other three words cannot be followed by the adjective 'sunburnt'.
10 D: the other words do not collocate with 'weather'.
11 C: the other words describe different movements.
12 B: the other linking words and phrases cannot be used here.

Part 2: Penguins on the move
13 out (preposition) 'coming out' contrasts with 'in their burrows'
14 which (relative pronoun) non-defining clause
15 since (adverbial) part of the linking phrase 'Ever since'
16 as (adverbial) part of the linking phrase 'as if'
17 (Al)though/While/Whilst (linker) provides a contrast
18 how (determiner) means 'in which way'
19 like (verb) means 'similar to'
20 however (linker) makes a contrast
21 when(ever)/if (linker) means 'every time'
22 in (preposition) part of the fixed phrase 'in search of'

23 is (verb) part of passive construction meaning 'people think'
24 have (auxiliary verb) part of compound tense

Part 3: The sky at night
25 mountainous: noun to adjective
26 pollution: verb to noun
27 fortunate: noun to adjective
28 impressive: verb to noun
29 height: adjective to noun
30 uninterrupted: verb to negative adjective
31 powerful: noun to adjective
32 discovery: verb to noun
33 existence: verb to noun
34 probability: adjective to noun

Part 4
35 is the price: verb 'to be' with article
36 is being opened: passive form
37 looking forward to: fixed expression
38 been my intention to: verb to noun
39 didn't mean to damage: fixed negative expression
40 to play tennis unless Fiona: infinitive after reporting verb, position of 'unless'
41 is expected to arrive: passive form
42 (which) Ralph found most exciting: comparative adjective after 'found'

The total score is adjusted to give a mark out of 20.

Test 1, Paper 4: Listening (page 18)

Part 1
1 B 2 C 3 B 4 C 5 A 6 C 7 C 8 C

Part 2: Sailing solo across the Atlantic
9 5600 / five thousand six hundred
10 *Cheeky Monkey*
11 (large/big) ships
12 tins
13 (hot) toast
14 binoculars
15 iPod
16 flying fish
17 'Children in Need'
18 photo(graph)s

Part 3
19 C 20 F 21 A 22 E 23 D

Part 4
24 B 25 B 26 C 27 C 28 A 29 B 30 A

The total score is adjusted to give a mark out of 20.

Test 2, Paper 1: Reading (page 24)

Part 1: Extract from a novel
1 B: 'I was really impressed … initially, thinking we'd finally found the true countryside.'

2 B: A ridge is a type of hill.
3 A: 'The only field that went with the farmhouse was the one beside the track.'
4 C: 'they hardly had any furniture in them'.
5 B: 'I don't think I really understood at that point what she was doing …'
6 B: 'I wasn't sure what damp was supposed to do to you, but I knew it wasn't good.'
7 C: 'it' refers to 'each' photograph.
8 D: 'Also it was free, so I realised it couldn't be up to much.'

Part 2: Bottlenose whales, the deep divers of the North Atlantic

9 H: Link between 'from a distance' and 'come closer'
10 A: Link between 'most of us wouldn't recognise' and 'least familiar'
11 F: Link between 'reach ten metres', 'they weigh …' and 'these basic facts'. Link between 'northern bottlenoses' and 'These are …'
12 G: Link between 'breaths like great sighs sound' and 'strange noises'. Link between 'four creatures' and 'The smallest one …'
13 C: Link between 'heads … pointing our way.' and 'aren't just watching us'. Link between 'aren't just …' and 'We are being studied …'
14 E: Link between 'may function as' and 'The same holds …'
15 B: Link between 'first solid data', 'a depth of 900 metres' and 'This revelation …'

Part 3: Women referees

16 B: 'so focussed … she didn't have time …'
17 C: 'knowing too it would be her final …'
18 A: 'I was sure I wouldn't make a wrong decision'
19 D: 'they can hear my voice …'
20 C: 'Factors included in the assessment …'
21 D: 'I have worked … to defeat this perception'
22 A: 'once they saw me on the field …, they would start …'
23 B: 'hoping to open doors for others to follow'
24 B: 'I don't think that people realise …'
25 D: 'I almost bounced myself out of the taxi'
26 B: 'The one group … I haven't had a single problem with …'
27 A: 'in sharp contrast to how she is on the field'
28 C: 'for umpires only personal satisfaction …'
29 A: 'needs to improve on her … Boys play very fast …'
30 D: 'My firm is very supportive, though'

The total score is adjusted to give a mark out of 20.

Test 2, Paper 2: Writing (page 30)

Part 1

Question 1
Style: formal
Content: 1 the kind of transport
2 what other information is needed
3 whether breakfast, lunch and dinner are provided
4 mention of sports

Part 2

Question 2
Style: informal
Content: 1 inexpensive/free music events available
2 visits to museums and reasons for choices
3 how to make the most of the time

Question 3
Style: formal or neutral
Content: 1 comment on the songs
2 description of the musicians
3 the school as a venue

Question 4
Style: semi-formal or neutral
Content: 1 what happened
2 how it ended

Question 5(a)
Style: formal
Content: reasons why the character is not pleasant
ways at least two characters were affected, with specific examples

Question 5(b)
Style: formal or neutral
Content: aspects of the book that make it suitable or unsuitable for teenagers
reasons for your opinions with reference to plot, characters, etc

The total score is adjusted to give a mark out of 40.

Test 2, Paper 3: Use of English (page 32)

Part 1: Sudoku
1 B: The other linking expressions can't be followed by 'you're not'.
2 C: The other words don't fit the context of the sentence.
3 C: The other verbs do not mean anything in the gap.
4 D: The other verbs to not make a phrasal verb with 'for'.
5 A: This is a very common collocation.
6 D: Only the right answer makes full sense in the context.
7 B: The other words do not collocate with 'worked'.
8 B: The phrasal verb 'taken off' is the only one that fits the context.
9 C: The other words do not take the preposition 'from'.
10 B: The other words cannot be followed by 'it as'.
11 A: The other words are not used to mean 'someone visiting a website'.

12 D: The phrasal verb 'coming up with' is the only one that fits the context.

Part 2: The birth of *YouTube*
13 how (determiner) gives the idea of degree
14 with (preposition) part of the phrasal verb
15 it (pronoun) part of fixed expression
16 set (verb) part of the phrasal verb
17 out (preposition) part of the phrasal verb
18 would/might (modal verb)
19 than (conjunction) joins 'more' to a quantity
20 of (preposition) part of fixed expression
21 been (verb) passive form
22 on (preposition) part of fixed expression
23 which (relative pronoun) introduces a clause
24 other (adverbial) part of linking phrase

Part 3: Putting the fun back into driving
25 pleasure: verb to noun
26 density: adjective to noun
27 growth: verb to noun
28 safety: adjective to noun
29 introduction: verb to noun
30 motorists: noun to plural noun
31 performance: verb to noun
32 enjoyment: verb to noun
33 popularity: adjective to noun
34 variety: verb to noun

Part 4
35 was not as difficult: comparative phrase with 'as'
36 advised Leon to tell: reporting verb with infinitive
37 a small number of people: parallel expression
38 years since Naomi (last) saw: change of subject and tense with 'since'
39 took part in: parallel phrasal verb
40 as long as you are: fixed phrase with present indicative
41 (that) she had chosen: past perfect after 'wished'
42 see the point in/of recycling: parallel expression with the noun

The total score is adjusted to give a mark out of 20.

Test 2, Paper 4: Listening (page 38)

Part 1
1 A **2** C **3** B **4** A **5** C **6** A **7** B **8** B

Part 2: The mysterious monster
9 sheep
10 surgeon's
11 boat
12 fine/good
13 publicity
14 photography
15 submarine
16 dolphins
17 flipper
18 plants/animals (in either order)

Part 3: Concerts
19 F **20** C **21** A **22** D **23** B

Part 4: Balloon trips
24 C **25** A **26** B **27** B **28** C **29** A **30** C

The total score is adjusted to give a mark out of 20.

Test 3, Paper 1: Reading (page 44)

Part 1: Travelling to learn
1 B: 'Three years … later … my conversational skills were limited to …'
2 B: 'but two little words always stopped me: home stay.'
3 D: 'misgivings' means doubts and refers to the previous paragraph.
4 C: 'wondering what I've let myself in for.'
5 A: 'one of us is a bit alarmed … another is disconcerted …'
6 D: 'daunting' means hard to face up to.
7 B: 'feckless' means not very hard-working.'
8 C: the tone of the whole penultimate paragraph is humorous, showing the writer's amusement

Part 2: If you're happy, the robot knows it
9 B: Link between 'the user changes position' and 'When you hang your head and …'
10 G: Link between 'its creators' and 'they'. Link between 'people' and 'them'
11 D: Link between 'is nothing new' and 'Researchers … have already proved …'
12 A: Link between 'foster greater attention' and 'provoke a greater response'. Link between the question and 'To find out, …'
13 F: Link between 'influence over the volunteers' and 'actually prompted lots of participants'
14 H: Link between 'use in the classroom' and 'meetings and classes'. Link between 'Hiroshi Ishiguro' and 'he has begun …'
15 E: Link between 'not universally accepted' and 'cannot protect the group' and 'this can be resolved'

Part 3: Wild camping
16 B: '… the excitement that comes from making yourself … vulnerable'
17 C: 'In less paranoid times, … but people nowadays …'
18 A: 'the only expense is feeding yourself' [18/19 in either order]
19 D: 'they don't cost that much'
20 B: 'ended up sharing the tiny uncomfortable tent …'
21 C: 'not keen to suggest good places …'
22 D: 'managed to pass on some of my enthusiasm …'
23 C: 'when it comes to feeling at ease with … kids are doing'
24 C: 'when apart from … a compass'
25 B: 'the experience put me off wild camping for months'
26 A: 'are waking up to the fact …'
27 D: 'somebody had failed to extinguish a small fire …'

28 C: 'I'd advise places which aren't too far from civilisation ...'

29 A: '... you can seldom escape the constant chattering ... or worse still, ...'

30 B: 'I must have a folding chair, a thin ... mattress ...'

Test 3, Paper 2: Writing (page 50)

Part 1

Question 1
Style: formal
Content: 1 request for information about number of students at advanced level
2 request for information about intensive courses
3 request for information about activities
4 reasons for wanting to stay with a family

Part 2

Question 2
Style: formal
Content: 1 description of favourite sport
2 age, reasons for starting, who you played with, etc
3 how it would help make friends

Question 3
Style: formal
Content: 1 what the comedy show is about
2 what parts made you laugh most, and why
3 whether the comedians were good actors, and why you think so
4 reasons for recommending it (or not) to other students

Question 4
Style: informal
Content: 1 what the summer job is, how much or how little you like it, whether you find it difficult to work when other people are on holiday
2 free time and wages

Question 5(a)
Style: formal
Content: agreement or disagreement with reasons and examples from the book

Question 5(b)
Style: informal or neutral
Content: description of a character which made an impression on you
references to his/her personality, looks, behaviour, influence on other characters, etc

The total score is adjusted to give a mark out of 40.

Test 3, Paper 3: Use of English (page 52)

Part 1: Boots for Africa
1 C: 'joined forces with' is a common expression.
2 B: The other words cannot be followed by 'as'.
3 D: The other words cannot be followed by 'of'.
4 A: The other words cannot be followed by 'in'.
5 B: 'set up' is a phrasal verb meaning 'to start'.
6 B: The other words do not collocate with 'support'.
7 C: The other words do not collocate with 'beneficial'.
8 D: Options A/C can't be used with this punctuation.
9 C: The other words do not collocate with 'good'.
10 A: The other words need a preposition.
11 D: The other words do not collocate with 'a donation'.
12 B: The other words do not collocate with 'information'.

Part 2: An influencial cook
13 for (preposition) to give idea of period of time
14 been (verb) present perfect passive form
15 rather (adverbial) part of contrastive expression
16 when (adverbial) time marker
17 that/which (relative pronoun) introduces a clause
18 more (adjective) part of linking expression
19 at (preposition) part of expression denoting quantity
20 in (preposition) part of expression indicating quantity
21 to (preposition) used after the verb 'to devote'
22 some (quantifier) to indicate a partial quantity
23 but (conjunction) introduces a contrastive clause
24 however/though (linker) introduces a contrast

Part 3: Young artists on display
25 especially: adjective to adverb
26 exhibition: verb to noun
27 traditionally: noun to adverb
28 tourists: noun to plural noun
29 wonderful: verb to adjective
30 pride: adjective to noun
31 accompany: noun to verb
32 favourite: verb to adjective
33 effective: noun to adjective
34 enthusiastic: noun to adjective

Part 4
35 off in case David: negative preposition with 'in case'
36 were given a map by: active to passive form
37 told me not to touch: direct to reported speech
38 a faster typist: verb to noun in a positive context
39 is unlikely to last: key word plus infinitive in present indicative
40 has difficulty in answering: key word plus preposition in positive context
41 had better leave: fixed phrase plus infinitive
42 Patty forgot to pack was: key word plus infinitive plus past tense verb

Test 3, Paper 4: Listening (page 58)

Part 1
1 A **2** B **3** A **4** C **5** A **6** A **7** C **8** B

Part 2: History of roller skating
9 Holland
10 violin
11 (large) mirror
12 *Winter Pleasures*
13 direction
14 (roller) hockey
15 championships
16 design/performance (in either order)
17 eight million/8,000,000 people
18 lighter/safer (in either order)

Part 3: First year at university
19 D   20 B   21 C   22 A   23 F

Part 4: Film actor
24 B   25 C   26 A   27 B   28 C   29 C   30 A

Test 4, Paper 1: Reading (page 64)

Part 1: Brighton Institute of Modern Music
1 B: This is the gist of the whole first paragraph.
2 C: 'We own it, and we set the culture'
3 A: The information about contracts in the next sentence supports this.
4 D: 'cash cows' are things that produce money for you – in this case the artists.
5 B: '… the main thing for me is the live performance events.'
6 D: This is supported by the fact that they didn't 'engage with school'.
7 C: 'It's a bit like a football team here, with people fulfilling different roles.'
8 A: 'many' (of them) are the tutors mentioned in the previous sentence.

Part 2: Femi Kuti, a great African musician
9 C: Link between 'his father' and 'his father's long shadow'. Link between 'a fine performer in his own right' and 'bringing his own unique creativity'
10 G: Link between 'his … son' and 'giving him'. Link between 'any signs of approval' and 'refused to give him any lessons'
11 A: Link between 'failed to make it on to the plane' and 'fill his place'. Link between 'did so, … with considerable skill' and 'This gave him the confidence …'
12 E: Link between 'Femi's debut album' and 'Now a collector's item, its mix of …'
13 B: Link between 'album … which earned him very good reviews' and 'It also won …' Link between 'reconciliation with his father' and 'He finally admitted …'
14 H: Link between 'he learnt things from him' and 'he taught me to be different'
15 F: Link between 'Femi's own son' and 'that's the advice I've given my own child'

Part 3: Anyone for extreme sports?
16 B: 'I had forgotten my first important lesson …'
17 D: 'returning to the sport might be like riding a bike …'

18 A: 'I'd no doubt be able to take my body weight …'
19 B: 'I did so and my more relaxed style …'
20 C: 'my co-trainees were all scuba divers'
21 A: 'I am now a fearless trapeze flyer'
22 D: 'My instructor had said they were not applicable …'
23 C: 'the best place in the world to learn …'
24 B: 'I know I'll feel completely at ease eventually'
25 A: 'all of a sudden I noticed a slight fluttering in my stomach'
26 D: 'What a thrill to feel the cool air …'
27 C: '… not so risky. When practised correctly …'
28 C: 'My partner … had trouble … Then I dived, … reached … easily'
29 A: 'a real feeling of regret when the … told me to stop'
30 B: 'I turned up fully kitted-up … which was embarrassing …'

Test 4, Paper 2: Writing (page 70)

Part 1

Question 1
Style: informal
Content: 1   how working could help
2   jobs and reasons why they are suitable or unsuitable
3   wages
4   accommodation

Part 2

Question 2
Style: formal
Content: 1   reasons for wanting to attend the course
2   description of musical skills and experience/favourite music

Question 3
Style: semi-formal or neutral
Content: 1   description of the cartoon/cartoon characters
2   what makes it funny, and why it may or may not appeal to older people

Question 4
Style: formal or neutral
Content: what happened to Harry: an introduction, development of the story and suitable conclusion

Question 5(a)
Style: formal
Content: details of plot, characters, events, message, style, etc, to back up opinions

Question 5(b)
Style: informal or neutral
Content: what makes the plot and the characters thrilling/interesting

The total score is adjusted to give a mark out of 40.

Test 4, Paper 3: Use of English
(page 72)

Part 1: Lunch is for sharing
1 C: The key is the correct term in the context of websites.
2 B: The other words don't collocate with 'record'.
3 C: The other words can't be followed by 'of'.
4 B: The key is part of a common expression.
5 D: The other words can't be followed by 'as'.
6 A: The others words can't be followed by 'of'.
7 B: The other words can't be used after 'in'.
8 A: The other words do not make sense in the context.
9 D: The other words can't be used with this punctuation.
10 C: The other words don't collocate with 'to understand'.
11 B: 'health conscious' is a common collocation.
12 A: The other words can't be followed by 'on'.

Part 2: Mr Bean
13 in (preposition) 'in length' is an expression indicating time or distance
14 Since (adverbial) part of a linking expression indicating a period of time
15 more (quantifier) 'more than' indicates a larger quantity
16 well (adjective) part of comparative phrase
17 by (preposition) collocates with 'played' to mean 'acted by'
18 (Al)though/While/Whilst (linker) introduces a contrastive clause
19 as (adverbial) part of fixed expression meaning 'called'
20 to (preposition) part of fixed expression indicating opinion
21 his (pronoun) 'own' with this meaning always has a personal pronoun
22 who (relative pronoun) introduces a clause
23 around (preposition) links idea to personal pronoun
24 such (adverbial) part of fixed expression used to indicate an example

Part 3: Computer games
25 influential: noun to adjective
26 creative: verb to adjective
27 impressive: verb to adjective
28 development: verb to noun
29 musicians: noun to plural noun
30 similarity: adjective to noun
31 economists: noun to plural noun
32 explanation: verb to noun
33 unexpected: adjective to negative adjective
34 personal: noun to adjective

Part 4
35 the most interesting place: change of form of adjective and syntax
36 flight had been on time: conditional with past perfect
37 they were grateful for: reporting verb plus adjectival phrase and preposition
38 not read your email unless: negative verb plus unless
39 wishes she hadn't lent: past perfect after 'wish'
40 must/will have been really disappointed: passive form with adjective
41 turned down Alex's: phrasal verb with possessive form of name
42 always my ambition to: possessive pronoun plus key word plus preposition

Test 4, Paper 4: Listening (page 78)

Part 1
1 C 2 C 3 B 4 C 5 B 6 C 7 A 8 A

Part 2: TV researcher
9 biology
10 media studies
11 Costa Rica
12 twelve
13 frog
14 waterfall
15 tuna
16 torch
17 'Sun Gun'
18 scared

Part 3: Craft workers
19 B 20 D 21 F 22 A 23 E

Part 4: Monica Darcey
24 A 25 B 26 B 27 C 28 A 29 C 30 B

Test 5, Paper 1: Reading (page 84)

Part 1
1 C: 'The things you worry about don't always turn out as badly as you expect. Sometimes they're worse.'
2 B: 'I'd got a special cheap offer on the Internet. But that was silly because Ruth's aunt was paying our expenses'
3 A: 'While I signed for the car – gripping the pen hard so that my name wouldn't look as shaky as I felt'
4 D: Ruth is referring back to the narrator's question.
5 B: 'lights would blaze round a corner ahead, without warning, looking as though they were coming right at us.'
6 C: 'It's right opposite a white house with green shutters, just like the directions say.'
7 B: 'scrunching' is the noise made by walking or driving over loose stones
8 D: 'I can't make the key work' … The lock had been changed. Very recently.

Part 2: Sparkling trainers
9 F: Link between 'far away from the red carpets' and 'It's an appropriate setting'. Link between 'Glasgow in Scotland' and 'home to a thriving …'
10 C: Link between 'something unique' and 'so like one another'. Link between 'something that nobody else has got' and 'that's precisely what Pauline is offering'

11 A: Link between 'Adidas and Puma trainers' and 'A shoe-shop manager … saw them'
12 H: Link between 'a few well-known people' and 'One of them … was photographed'. Link between 'couldn't believe my luck' and 'It was amazing!'
13 B: Link between 'who do you turn for help?' and 'I went to the Prince's Scottish Youth Business Trust'
14 E: Link between 'is slightly uneasy' and 'someone else … is a worry', and 'Some people started selling … similar to mine'
15 G: Link between 'I do get a bit stressed' and 'But I never get bored'

Part 3: Thinking of a career in tourism?
16 B: 'There's a shortage of first-class chefs …'
17 C: 'allow people to do what they want, while at the same time making sure …
18 B: 'Had I taken a full-time college course … I would have …'
19 D: 'crucial to be able to exercise good judgment …'
20 A: 'not to be put off by … low wages at the start'
21 E: 'the manager soon realised she had the skills …'
22 B: 'though these advantages are more likely to come from …'
23 A: 'the right degree … is no guarantee …'
24 C D: 'a holidaymaker spotted some incorrect details …' (C/D in either order)
25 C D: 'Once, I forgot to give somebody a life jacket …'
26 A C: '… allows her to continue with her degree …' (A/C in either order)
27 A C: 'attend regular local history classes'
28 E: 'hoping to be able to start my own …'
29 D: 'educational institutions are only just beginning to …'
30 E: 'The job outlook isn't good right now'

Test 5, Paper 2: Writing (page 90)

Part 1

Question 1
Style: Formal. Complain and correct the information in a polite manner.
Content: 1 Explain the information about the speaker being ill was available.
   2 Mention the qualifications of the speaker.
   3 Argue that the age of the speaker is not so important.
   4 Give information about next week's talk.

Part 2

Question 2
Style: formal
Content: 1 Say in what way you are good at working with people.
   2 Explain what you can do in English and/or other languages you know.
   3 Say you can work flexible hours.
   4 Give any other reasons why you would be suitable for this job.

Question 3
Style: semi-formal or formal
Content: Remember the main purpose of a review is to give a personal opinion. You must give the reader a clear impression of the quality of what you are reviewing.
   1 Describe some of the characters and say why they are interesting (e.g. true to life, varied, good-looking, etc).
   2 Say why you watch it regularly and explain why you would or would not recommend it to everone.

Question 4
Style: formal or neutral
Content: Describe how Maria felt and what happened after she decided to ask for help. Who did she ask? What were the consequences? Decide how your story is going to develop and end before you start writing.

Question 5(a)
Style: formal
Content: Include examples of occasions when the character you have chosen is treated unfairly or misunderstood. Give reasons for your opinions. Say how the character reacts when treated in this way.

Question 5(b)
Style: Formal. This is a report, so it is advisable to use headings.
Content: Deal with each point in turn. The characters: who they are. Are they interesting for teenagers? The topic: explain what it is and say if it is suitable for the age group. The plot: summarise the plot. Is it complex or easy to follow? Why?

The total score is adjusted to give a mark out of 20.

Test 5, Paper 3: Use of English (page 92)

Part 1: The world's finest chocolates
1 B: The other words do not make sense in the context.
2 A: The other words do not make sense in the context.
3 D: The other words do not give the idea of a list.
4 C: The other words do not collocate with 'regarded'.
5 B: 'Picking up' is a phrasal verb which means 'collecting'.
6 B: Options A/D do not make sense and option C would need a preposition.
7 D: The other options cannot be used with 'than'.
8 B: The other options would not make an expression that introduces an idea.
9 C: The other words do not collocate with 'selection'.
10 A: The other words do not collocate with 'view'.
11 A: The other options would need an object (e.g. 'us').

12 C: The other options do not make the common expression.

Part 2: Health on holiday
13 a/any/much (quantifier) to indicate degree
14 well (adverbial) completes the set expression
15 is (verb) precedes the main subject of the sentence
16 that/which (relative pronoun) introduces further information about the kit
17 on/forth (preposition) completes the expression meaning 'etcetera'
18 out (preposition) 'sorted out' is a phrasal verb meaning 'solved'
19 in (preposition) completes the fixed expression
20 how (determiner) means 'in what way'
21 more (adverbial) combines with 'much' to give idea of degree
22 what (determiner) links two infinitives
23 case (noun) completes the linking phrase 'in case'
24 a (article) completes the set expression

Part 3: Music and maths
25 Unfortunately: adverb to negative adverb
26 occasionally: noun to adverb
27 performances: verb to plural noun
28 movement: verb to noun
29 endless: noun to negative adjective
30 connection: verb to noun
31 references: verb to plural noun
32 fascination: verb to noun
33 relationship: concrete noun to abstract noun
34 boredom: verb to noun

Part 4
35 was the first time (that): past tense plus common expression
36 from Luca, all (of): preposition plus positive idea
37 has no objection to: collocation plus noun from verb
38 (that) I get very bored: new subject plus different form of adjective
39 is supposed to be: passive form
40 they would rather: conditional tense
41 was not allowed while/whilst: passive voice plus time reference
42 if the machine had been: third conditional with past perfect tense

Test 5, Paper 4: Listening (page 98)

Part 1
1 C **2** C **3** C **4** B **5** C **6** A **7** B **8** C

Part 2: The peacock
9 fan
10 India
11 four thousand/4000
12 neck
13 eyes
14 brown
15 proud
16 water

17 sleep
18 crocodiles

Part 3: First novels
19 E **20** B **21** F **22** C **23** A

Part 4: Professional ceramicist
24 C **25** B **26** A **27** B **28** A **29** A **30** C

Test 6, Paper 1: Reading (page 104)

Part 1: Assistants to the stars
1 B: 'he was initially reluctant to talk to me because I was a journalist'
2 C: 'were still widely sought after'
3 A: 'he's looking to unwind in front of the television after a long day's work'
4 C: 'Without wasting another minute, he picks up the phone …'
5 D: 'Holder told Johnson that he should consider …'
6 B: 'was extremely courageous – there's no denying that'
7 C: A 'perk' is an additional benefit of doing a job (i.e. as well as the salary).
8 A: 'being an assistant was not the means to an end but an end in itself'

Part 2: Cayman Brac and Little Cayman
9 E: Link between 'lovers of the outdoors' and 'They'. Link between 'outdoors' and 'the walking and the cycling'. Link between 'diving' and 'divers'
10 H: Link between '300 metres' and 'down this far…'
11 F: Link between 'not really built up apart from …' and 'this lack of development …'
12 A: Link between 'coral reef' and 'It starts … and … plunges …'
13 D: Link between 'not just about the sea' and 'Back on land …'
14 G: Link between 'is quite different' and 'it is much livelier'
15 B: Link between 'migrating birds' and 'As well as these visitors …'

Part 3: The bestsellers
16 D: 'by offering customers that special … touch'
17 A: 'This shop is also an information centre'
18 C: 'she admits she does not know how … her profits'
19 B: 'making his shop window eye-catching … It is … important'
20 C: 'fashionable part of the city, but then discovered …'
21 D: 'I offer lots of discounts, but not on …'
22 A: 'It'll be hard to find somebody … to invest …'
23 C: 'sat in the cafés and listened to conversations …'
24 B: 'disparity in quality … the people … helping the customer … don't feel valued'
25 D: 'I was having a conversation … I said I would have …'
26 A: 'We carry a vast range … show children the way …'
27 B: 'mostly university students and young professionals'

28 C: 'I've got a pretty good idea of what's in most of them'

29 D: 'a space upstairs for author talks and …'

30 A: 'buyers from the area are loyal …'

Test 6, Paper 2: Writing (page 110)

Part 1

Question 1

Style: formal or neutral

Content:
1 Say that you are keen to find an exciting holiday.
2 Express an interest in whitewater rafting, mention your lack of experience and find out about lessons.
3 Give information about the length of your stay and the sports you want, and explain you do not want to do anything too dangerous.
4 Ask whether travel insurance is included.

Part 2

Question 2

Style: Formal. Use clear paragraphs.

Content: You may agree, disagree, or partially agree. You may want to include some of the following points: what music you can download, why people download music (quick, cheap, fun, etc), what equipment/permission, etc is needed, the effect of downloading on high-street shops, whether shops offer any special service. Your last paragraph must be a clear conclusion where you summarise the arguments you have presented.

Question 3

Style: formal

Content: Remember the main purpose of a review is to give a personal opinion. You must give the reader a clear impression of the quality of what you are reviewing.
1 Describe the programme and say why it is interesting (e.g. natural beauty, wild animals, commentary, colour, etc).
2 Explain why you think the programme is (un)suitable for children as well as adults.

Question 4

Style: Formal. Use headings.

Content: You may want to devide your report into Books, Magazines and DVDs. Under each heading, refer to the type of material teenagers might like, e.g. under 'Books': horror fiction, natural history, art books, etc. Explain why you think these materials would be popular.

Question 5(a)

Style: informal

Content: You may agree or disagree with your friend, or agree in some respects. You need to give reasons and examples from the book to back up your opinions.

Question 5(b)

Style: formal

Content: You have to give a brief description of the two characters and highlight the conflicts between them. Then say whether all or some of these conflicts are resolved at the end.

The total score is adjusted to give a mark out of 40.

Test 6, Paper 3: Use of English (page 112)

Part 1: My first expedition

1 C: The other words cannot be followed by 'in'.
2 B: The other words are not preceded by 'by'.
3 B: The other words cannot modify 'not'.
4 C: The other words do not complete the common expression.
5 A: 'drop out' is a phrasal verb that means 'withdraw from a commitment'.
6 D: The other words do not complete the common expression.
7 A: The other words do not collocate with 'doubts'.
8 D: The other words would need an object (e.g. 'to us').
9 A: The other words do not make sense in the context.
10 B: The other words are not followed by a gerund.
11 D: The other word do not complete the common expression.
12 C: The other words do not make sense in context.

Part 2: Shopping trolley joins the push for fitness

13 so (adverbial) part of the expression 'so called'
14 which/that (relative pronoun) introduces more information about the trolley
15 into (preposition) the verb 'transform' is followed by this preposition
16 and (conjunction) completes the idea began with 'both'
17 are (verb) passive voice
18 with (preposition) introduces additional information
19 many (quantifier) completes the comparative phrase indicating degree
20 other (adjective) part of fixed linking expression
21 out (preposition) 'to point out' is a phrasal verb meaning 'to inform'
22 pay (verb) part of the common expression
23 what (determiner) introduces second idea in the sentence
24 when/if/once (linker) time marker that introduces a clause

Part 3: Toy story

25 carefully: adjective to adverb
26 collection: verb to noun
27 appearance: verb to noun
28 outfits: verb to plural compound noun
29 variety: verb to noun
30 fully: adjective to adverb
31 undamaged: adjective to negative adjective
32 investment: verb to noun
33 impressive: verb to adjective
34 working: verb to adjective

Part 4

35 as a surprise to Pete: fixed expression
36 never managed to win: verb plus infinitive
37 on our own: prepositional phrase
38 are not as serious as: comparative form
39 was still doing/finishing: positive continuous verb form with 'still'
40 were you, I would make: conditional form plus phrase instead of verb
41 my opinion it was: 'opinion' plus new subject
42 been living in Toronto since: present continuous plus preposition

Test 6, Paper 4: Listening (page 118)

Part 1
1 C 2 A 3 C 4 C 5 C 6 B 7 B 8 B

Part 2: The carbon coach
9 consultant
10 ecologist
11 bills
12 carbon meter
13 the government
14 light bulbs
15 (its/their) concerts
16 Earthship
17 (the) wind (power)
18 handbook

Part 3: Hill walking
19 E 20 F 21 A 22 B 23 D

Part 4: Trapeze artist
24 B 25 A 26 B 27 C 28 C 29 B 30 A

Tapescripts

Test 1, Paper 4: Listening, Part 1 (page 18)

You will hear people talking in eight different situations. For questions 1–8, choose the best answer (A, B or C).

1

Well, there are two campsites, about five kilometres apart, but I'd go to the Morvich site if I were you – unless you want to be near the castle and the museum, which are a fair distance from it even if you're driving. All we wanted was to be able to go for walks and enjoy the stunning views of the lake. You definitely wouldn't get that at the other site, though I've heard that the showers are better than at Morvich, and it's also got a little shop which you may find useful. We don't bother about things like that, so we'll definitely go back to Morvich next summer.

2

M: I've just got back from the Alps. Lots of the mountain passes that are normally full of snow at this time of year, are still green. If this is the result of global warming, it's very worrying.

F: There are certainly strange things happening to the weather, but there's nothing to worry about really. My sister spent two weeks in Cape Town last year, where she'd hoped to find big waves and plenty of wind to surf, and she was shocked to find nothing. I went two weeks ago and it was a completely different story.

M: I can't believe that you're saying that. There's no hope for our planet unless something's done soon.

3

W: You've got this idea that moving to the country's going to change your life dramatically, but it needn't be like that at all. I know you can't bear the thought of giving up simple things like going to the library or the gym, but think of all the …

M: You don't understand how important all that is for me.

W: Well, the main thing is your job wouldn't be affected, you'd be able to carry on writing your articles anywhere, wouldn't you?

M: From the point of view of work it might not be a bad thing, there'd be no interruptions from well-meaning friends dropping in for a chat any time of day.

4

This afternoon I'll be joined by Phil Harkins, the chef whose cookery books and television appearances have made him a celebrity. But this time instead of talking about his award-winning books or his TV cookery courses, he'll be helping you. You may have learnt how to cook at home, or at school, or maybe you went to a cookery school. But are you still unsure about a few things? Phil will try to clarify any doubts you may still have, so whether it's how to cook the perfect boiled egg or how to organise a five course meal, now's your chance. Call us from three o'clock.

5

A team of nutritionists has been evaluating the food which is on sale in a number of college canteens, with surprising results. The survey shows that the increased variety of snacks on offer is remarkable, though the situation's still far from ideal. It wasn't long ago that there were constant complaints about the lack of fruit and vegetables and the predominance of high sugar and fatty items, from teachers in particular. Probably as a result of that pressure, colleges became aware of the problem, without ever promising quick results. Perhaps not surprisingly, the students themselves say they miss the sweeter snacks.

6

I'd recently left school and I was helping my parents in their shop, when I heard about this half-day vacancy at the bookshop. The only work I'd ever done was a few hours at the shop and a few little holiday jobs, which were great fun because my friends were doing them too. But whilst I was a bit uneasy about this job because I'm not that good at admin tasks, I could see that this was my chance to focus on those weak points. I'd have made more money if I'd stayed working in the shop, as my parents were keen to point out, but I don't regret my choice.

7

M: A lot's been said about Jack Sommer, the young designer who's set to dominate next year's fashion shows with his bold designs in strong colours, hasn't it Jane?

F: Yes, Sommer's collections have been both praised to the sky and criticised harshly by the press, and it's not difficult to understand why this should be. He uses everyday materials, but for dresses that would be out of place anywhere except the catwalk. You can't imagine yourself wearing them, no matter how special the occasion. <u>But I believe this is precisely his strength. He's an artist who has created objects of beauty unlike any other.</u>

8

F: So how's it different to other winter sports?

M: Well, take downhill skiing, for instance. You have to book lessons, start on the nursery slopes and all that – <u>but with snow-kiting, you just need a wide, snow-covered area like a frozen lake or field, and you're off</u>. Like with all winter sports, beginners should err on the side of caution. They need to be sure they can judge wind speed.

Test 1, Paper 4: Listening, Part 2 (page 20)

You will hear a radio programme about a boy called Michael who crossed the Atlantic in a sailing boat. For questions 9–18, complete the sentences.

In 2007, Michael Perham, a fourteen-year-old boy from the south of England, became the youngest person to sail across the Atlantic alone. Michael set off from Gibraltar on <u>the 5600 kilometre voyage</u> which took forty-seven days. It was a long and, some may say, dangerous adventure, but Michael was determined to get there.

Michael started sailing when he was seven, and says the idea of an Atlantic crossing had been floating around in his head for a few years. Then one day, his father, Peter, who's a keen sailor, decided that the time was right. Michael helped with the design of a new 9-metre yacht which was built for them and <u>to which Michael gave the name *Cheeky Monkey*</u>.

They say that for a real sailor, crossing the Atlantic isn't a big deal, but people imagine that sharks and huge waves would be the greatest dangers. In fact, Michael's father sailed alongside his son in his own boat to make sure he was OK. They worked in shifts throughout the night; an hour on, then an hour off, because one of them had to be on watch, <u>in case large ships came too near to them</u>.

Are you wondering what Michael ate during his voyage? Well, he says he and his father filled two supermarket trolleys with things like sausages, spaghetti and stews, which could be easily heated in a pan. <u>Everything had to be in tins</u>, though, because that type of food keeps fresher than stuff in packets or jars.

So what did Michael miss most? He says he sometimes missed human contact and having a face-to-face conversation. He got used to his limited food supply but says what he <u>really longed for was hot toast</u>. Knowing what teenagers are like, I'd been expecting him to say burgers or crisps, but then Michael is no ordinary teenager!

When asked how he communicated with his father, Michael explains that it was all done by radio, <u>though for Michael nothing compared with the pleasure of following his father's progress</u> through his binoculars. Michael also communicated with his family at home by satellite phone. One day his father contacted Michael to tell him a part of his own boat was broken, which really disappointed Michael because it might mean that they would have to go slower. But, in the end, that wasn't necessary.

I asked Michael how he entertained himself on the boat. He told me he'd taken his guitar with him but it had stayed in its case throughout the trip. He couldn't play because the boat was always rolling about! He loved to read and <u>he also had an iPod that his sister had lent him</u>. This he plugged into portable speakers and it was on pretty much all the time.

Was there anything that frightened Michael? He says the weather was a bit of a worry at times, and once he got caught in a force-nine storm, but managed to handle the boat OK. <u>The one event that really shook him was when a flying fish jumped into the boat and hit him on the shoulder.</u> But mostly things were great, like sailing alongside dolphins and seeing the bluest skies anyone could ever imagine.

Everybody is really proud of Michael's achievements. And a remarkable thing about the trip is that he also raised thousands of pounds for <u>the charity known as 'Children in Need'</u>. His school has been very supportive – the headteacher allowed Michael to miss school, saying that a few weeks on the ocean would be an amazing learning experience.

It's quite likely that Michael's next challenge will be to sail non-stop around the world. His father would do the trip in another boat, but it would be a very different experience because they would be in 20-metre boats which travel much faster, so they would never really be in sight of each other. <u>Michael says next time he'll remember to pack some photos</u>, to remember friends and family if he feels lonely, but he'll leave the guitar at home!

You will hear five different people talking about cookery courses. For questions 19–23, choose from the list (A–F) what each speaker says about the course they took. Use the letters only once. There is one extra letter which you do not need to use.

Speaker 1

There's such a vast range of cookery schools, it's unbelievable. Before booking a course, it's advisable to decide what you want from it. For me it was easy – I wanted to pick up some new ideas for entertaining but didn't need any basic techniques, so the course at the Brandale cookery school suited me well. There were some people there who didn't know how to boil an egg, but there was extra tuition for them. The course is run by Sylvie Brandale, who's written cookbooks and appeared on TV, and subjects included 'Stress-free parties' and 'Sauces from around the world'. All great topics and all of the ingredients were provided.

Speaker 2

I was very lucky, really. I was on holiday, and I happened to hear that there was a new cookery school at the nearby Four Seasons Hotel. They had four-hour classes every Saturday, starting at 7 am! The day I attended there was a group of ten enthusiastic participants, all eagerly awaiting instructions – though I gathered from their conversations that, unlike me, they were all fairly experienced cooks. You can imagine the look on our faces though when we were told we were going to visit the open-air fish market down by the port. We all came back having selected freshly caught seafood, and were then taught the art of preparing it. Great stuff!

Speaker 3

I'm a good cook, or so my sister says. So she thought I'd do an advanced course. But I was keen to go through the basics again, and this time I was determined to enjoy it. I registered for Glyn Harvey's cookery classes – only four people in a class. We watched while he prepared the dishes, making it all seem so effortless! There wasn't much real cooking, although he did invite us to help slice the potatoes and tomatoes. And we were given some tasty, easy-to-cook recipes to take home. I came away bursting with ideas for giving a dinner party – something I hadn't felt like doing in a long time.

Speaker 4

The course I attended covered a range of techniques, from basic to advanced, and it gave you lots of practical tips. I was there to make up for the fact that, sadly, as a youngster, I was hardly ever allowed into the kitchen, which meant I'd turned into a chuck-it-in-the-pan sort of cook. Claire, the teacher, was very chatty and full of enthusiasm. She demonstrated several dishes in the morning while we took notes, and then we were given some equipment and it was our turn to have a go. I made a splendid vegetable tart, which we ate at lunch. Now I'm planning to go again and this time I'll concentrate on the more demanding recipes.

Speaker 5

This weekend cookery course I did, had an emphasis on local ingredients, with hands-on practice with the chefs. I wouldn't have been happy with taking notes and following demonstrations, no matter how impressive the food produced. I wanted to get my hands dirty, just as I'd done as a little girl in school cookery lessons. It was at a seaside resort, and you stay in a hotel which is very close to the fishing port, and so get to cook the local seafood. It's really intensive and you cook two-course lunches as well as four-course dinners! But you get enough free time to make it an enjoyable weekend too.

You will hear an interview with Pamela Green, a young fashion designer. For questions 24–30, choose the best answer (A, B or C).

Interviewer: Hello, Pamela, welcome to the programme. So many young people want to be fashion designers these days, but don't know how to get started.

Pamela Green: Hi. I felt exactly like that myself! You must first discover if this is really what you want to do. I wasn't sure to begin with, so I started off by looking for a store in my neighbourhood that sold its own clothes. The owner invited me into her studio and told me what a typical day was like. She allowed me to ask as many questions as I wanted. Having made up my mind, I then contacted a few colleges to see what courses in fashion were on offer, and I was lucky to find one that seemed ideal.

Interviewer: So a degree in fashion is a must?

Pamela Green: Well, you often meet designers who go to college later in life, after years of working in the industry. The truth is the best students aren't always the best designers, but there's no denying that a degree will show that you've got certain basic skills and get you your first job. Don't be surprised to find colleagues with fewer qualifications on higher pay than yourself though. Making progress from that point will depend entirely on your personal talent.

Interviewer: What basic skills do you need?

Pamela Green: When you ask a fashion student what they want to do, they often reply 'have my own line'. Not an easy task, I must say. You need work experience first, ideally in a successful fashion shop, to understand that this industry is led by commerce. Starting your own line requires capital and a clear overview of how it's going to develop. Without it, clothes design can only be a hobby. Of course, if you've got an eye for colour, style and shape and an ability to draw, you shouldn't let go of the dream.

Interviewer: Where do you get the inspiration for your designs?

Pamela Green: To be a good designer, you have to be aware of the world you live in, you need to go out and look at people's lives and attitudes, you really have to learn how to observe what's happening around you. And I don't mean going abroad necessarily – my social circle is invaluable for me, for example – a constant source of ideas. You have to remember the clothes are not for you, you have to adapt to what other people want. And don't be tempted to imitate the famous designers, however beautiful their collections might look.

Interviewer: Now you're a successful designer, are things easier?

Pamela Green: It took me a while to learn to cope with criticism, though. You think your design drawings look brilliant, but you mustn't get upset if the garment doesn't look as you'd imagined it. What I've never managed to get used to is the sheer amount of work involved in finishing your collection well in advance of the season. Some designers stop attending fashion shows, for example, which involve lots of time-consuming travelling, but I'd be unhappy to give that up.

Interviewer: Do you have to do a lot of reading to keep up with trends?

Pamela Green: You have to read fashion magazines and other media that reflect current trends and tastes. It doesn't matter whether you want to use them in your own designs. Nobody knows what styles will be fashionable in, say, two years' time, but the point is you have to know just about everything that's been done before, so that you can spot it when it becomes popular again.

Interviewer: This is a very competitive industry. Realistically, what are the chances for somebody starting?

Pamela Green: Don't make the mistake of aiming just for designing outfits, which is just one part of a vast industry. You may be perfectly happy as an obscure but competent designer of small pieces for collections – jewellery, hats, shoes – all of which need to be created. And then somebody has to market them, sell them, write about them. Fame and glory is just for the top twenty world designers, and life isn't always wonderful even for them.

Interviewer: Pamela, many thanks.

Test 2, Paper 4: Listening, Part 1 (page 38)

You will hear people talking in eight different situations. For questions 1–8, choose the best answer (A, B or C).

1
This was a one-week course, and I decided to go for it because at school I never had much time for art. I paid thirty pounds, which is reasonable when you consider that the materials are included. The thing is, although I didn't expect the teacher to do it all for me, I did at least expect some ideas about what to do, some useful tips, you know, like 'you should design your piece on paper first', which would've been useful. Anyway, the plate I produced didn't look very professional, but I made a great soap dish for my bathroom. I don't think the other students did much better.

2
With the summer approaching, and all this good weather we're having, it's time to start thinking of the outdoor life. Graham Sanders, who's an expert on mountain climbing, is going to be explaining how to make sure you get exactly the right kit. There's so many products now that finding the right items can be a difficult job. But by picking up some insider secrets you can be sure of making the right choice. And when you've got your gear home, it'll be time to show off all you can do! As Graham often says, with some preparation, anybody can climb even the highest mountain!

3
As soon as you start an exercise programme, you'll start looking healthier, and if you keep it up, you'll see the difference in the mirror within a few weeks. Forget the scales, they're not a good way of telling if you're losing body fat. Replacing fat with muscle makes you look better, but it may actually increase you weight, as muscle weighs more. So just look in the mirror and enjoy the improvement. And don't be fooled by the usual fad diets telling you to cut out

sugar or bread. None of them work and some people think they're downright dangerous.

4

F: Did you see the advert on the college noticeboard, about weekend jobs in the kitchens?

M: Yes, but I really wanted something that's related to my studies, you know, that would look good on my CV. Mind you, it would get me out of the house and give me something a bit less serious to do. And, of course, it would help to have the extra money, what with the fees and the books I need this term.

F: I'm lucky not to have that problem. But I like the idea of meeting people: that really sounds fun and I don't think we should be worrying about our career prospects yet.

5

M: Jane! Great to see you on your bike! So at last you've left your car at home!

F: Well, it's not for the reasons you think. I've put the car up for sale – on my student income, it just didn't work. I know, I know, don't start lecturing me about car fumes, the ozone layer, the polluted air we breathe … Look at the state I'm in after a quarter of an hour of cycling! Exhausted and cold, who knows, I might have caught flu or something.

M: If you're ill, you shouldn't be doing this of course.

F: Oh, don't worry. I'm sure I'll feel better when I warm up a bit.

6

Scrambling is often described as the grey area between walking and climbing – technically, as soon as you start to put your hands on rock, it becomes a scramble. However, one person's scrambling is another person's climbing – it depends on your perception. If you come from a walking background, as soon as your hand touches the ground you may class that as a scramble, whereas if you're from a climbing background, you'd think differently. The typical scramblers are people who find rock climbing too difficult or who don't have a head for heights.

7

Now for the weather in the north east for the rest of today and tomorrow. The spell of cold weather, brought in by arctic winds, is set to continue today,

with increasing cloud this afternoon, followed by snow showers in the evening. Tomorrow's looking more promising, with temperatures rising by two or three degrees as a result of a few more hours of sunshine, though the wind will remain strong, perhaps slightly less so than today, with gusts of up to 80 kilometres an hour in most areas. The severe weather's likely to continue well into next week.

8

And now some news about the Orion Theatre. The local council has decided to concentrate financial support on other venues in the city centre, after realising that the Orion would've needed about fourteen million pounds of investment to save it. An award-winning film-maker will make a 45-minute documentary which will follow the staff and production companies as the Orion Theatre enters its final season, including interviews with famous performers. The aim is to concentrate on the achievements of the theatre as a venue for arts in the local community since it first opened its doors in 1989, and on its reputation for innovative and creative theatre.

Test 2, Paper 4: Listening, Part 2 (page 40)

You will hear a talk on the radio about the Loch Ness Monster. For questions 9–18, complete the sentences.

Loch Ness, a large inland lake in Scotland, is one of the most famous tourist sites in the world – and this is not simply because of its stunning beauty. Mostly, it is because of the mystery of the 'Monster' that may hide in its waters. The Monster, known affectionately as Nessie, is said to have a huge, dark body and a long neck and its head has been described as small and similar to a sheep's. So, what is the actual evidence for its existence?

What captured people's imaginations in 1933 was the publication of a picture of the monster in a London newspaper. This photograph was called 'the surgeon's picture', because that was the profession of the man who took it. Many people had doubts about it, but the photo matched the descriptions of the monster by other eyewitnesses.

The best known film evidence for the creature is a cine film of something large moving at speed through the water. It was taken in 1960 by a man called Tim Dinsdale. It was shot from the mouth of a river which runs into Loch Ness from the south. Many critics said it was probably a boat, but when Dinsdale submitted the film for analysis by experts, they concluded that this was definitely not the case.

Tim Dinsdale thought that the monster was very probably a prehistoric animal, one that people believed to be extinct. On a more practical note, he discovered that sightings of Nessie tended to happen on fine days and that Nessie-spotting was a waste of time on windy or rainy days. However, if you visit Loch Ness, you'll see lots of tourists spending hours staring at the loch in any weather, in the hope of spotting the monster.

Undoubtedly, some sightings are the product of wishful thinking or the mistaken identification of objects on the loch. But for the most part, the accounts are those of honest people who insist they do not seek publicity but simply want to tell their amazing tale. With so many sightings, researchers eventually came to the conclusion that it would be worth spending the time and money needed to investigate it scientifically.

In 1962 the Loch Ness Investigation Bureau was set up, and in 1968 the first serious underwater investigation of the loch was launched. Up to that point, the only technology available had been photography, but now sonar equipment was available, which is the underwater equivalent of radar. Though there were some strong contacts with a large moving object, the results were inconclusive.

In 1969 a small private submarine came to the loch with the intention of firing darts at the creature to get a sample of its skin. But like many others before and since, this project was defeated by the poor visibility because the dirty waters of Loch Ness contain large amounts of peat, a type of black soil. This also explains why television cameras cannot be used down there.

So what else could be done? There was, for a time, a serious suggestion to bring in a number of dolphins to join the researchers, but it soon became clear that this was a non-starter. The obstacles would have been enormous, starting with the logistical problems of transporting them and then feeding them.

In 1972, new computer-enhancement techniques were introduced. Dr Robert Rines, of the Academy of Applied Science in Boston, succeeded in taking a picture which is now famous. Using a special flash, he photographed what appears to be the flipper of a huge animal. If it is, then it belongs to a creature unknown to science. Naturally this provoked a storm of controversy, which shows no signs of dying down.

So what's the latest? Using the most modern technology, there's now a project to investigate all the loch's plants and animals, some of which have probably never been seen due to the incredible depth of the water. But will the monster offer itself for examination? Who knows! For nearly 1500 years the legend of the Loch Ness monster has persisted and the elusive beast still continues to exert its magnetism across the world.

Test 2, Paper 4: Listening, Part 3 (page 41)

You will hear five different people talking about concerts they went to. For questions 19–23, choose from the list (A–F) the opinion each speaker expresses about the concert. Use the letters only once. There is one extra letter which you do not need to use.

Speaker 1
The concert went on for three hours and it featured a variety of bands. I'd have preferred something shorter and of higher quality, to be honest. The first band to come on, *The Beats*, didn't seem to have rehearsed their set very well. Nice catchy rhythms, but otherwise it was a mess. What made the evening worthwhile for me was the fact that all profits from ticket sales were going to a charity devoted to child care. There was a huge audience because you don't often get the chance to see so many bands at one venue, and only for a few dollars.

Speaker 2
This was a concert by *Brighton Club*, a great rock band just back from a successful tour of Latin America. But the first part was all new stuff – and a bit boring. And although everyone was shouting out the titles of songs they wanted to hear, the band took no notice, which was a shame. I mean it's a bit bad when you finally get the chance to see your favourite band live and then they refuse to play their best songs. Anyway, after a while, we all started getting into the new material and by the end the audience response was great. So I don't think anybody minded the forty dollars they'd paid.

Speaker 3
This was a concert by Celia Samson and her band, who play pop with some touches of jazz and country. She's got a beautiful voice, but the rest of the band let her down rather. At times it felt a bit like a high-school recital, with the audience clapping and cheering all the time when there was nothing much to shout about. All fine and good, except I don't particularly enjoy paying thirty dollars for a high-school performance where profits go to second-class musicians. Mind you, I've paid that kind of money in the past for concerts to help research, or to fight world poverty, but that's a different thing entirely.

Speaker 4
This was a concert by the Brenda Amis band. I wouldn't have wanted to miss the beginning – a huge cloud of smoke swelled on the stage, and out of it emerged Brenda Amis, with jet-black hair piled up with a feather and a big flower on top. I know some people would've wanted her to include her latest songs, <u>but I was happy enough that the night was all about the old favourites I've listened to so many times</u>. At the end, she had a short exchange with the audience: 'Thanks so much, guys. You're so nice.', and then she sang 'Only for Big Girls', and got a standing ovation.

Speaker 5
This was a gig by the *Sam Barnes Band*. Sam's my favourite guitarist right now. His approach to the instrument is the complete opposite to tradition – he'll hold the guitar upside down with the neck touching the ground. The music's punk and he's got a great band, particularly the bass player and the drummer. They've done some CDs, but <u>they've never yet made a record that really captures what they do on stage. You're less likely to be impressed by their recordings, but people were just stunned at the gig, it blew everybody's mind</u>. I only wished they'd played more of my favourite tracks, but you can't have everything.

You will hear an interview with Patrick Shaw, who works as a pilot for a company that organises hot-air balloon trips. For questions 24–30, choose the best answer (A, B or C).

Interviewer: In the studio today is Patrick Shaw, who is a hot-air balloon pilot. Patrick, would you say ballooning is a safe sport?

Patrick Shaw: Hi. Yes, a balloon's a very simple thing: when the air inside is heated, the balloon rises, and to descend, the pilot allows the air to cool. The pilot has complete control of the up-and-down movements. He may not know exactly where the balloon will land, but that doesn't mean he can't control <u>the landing, which is what people are most anxious about</u>. The fabric of the balloon is tough – if a bird were to fly into it, it would almost certainly bounce off.
Interviewer: What's the best way to start?

Patrick Shaw: Well, I started as a member of what's called 'ground crew'. That means the people who help with all aspects of the flight, from take-off to landing. It's a job which keeps you on the ground, <u>but it does allow you to see at first hand what balloon flight is all about</u>. That's why you do it, and for the fun – don't expect any money in return for your efforts until you become a pilot though. They're the only ones who make a living out of it.

Interviewer: So how difficult is it to become a member of the ground crew?

Patrick Shaw: The job of the ground crew is to assist the pilot. This includes setting up the balloon, and even talking to the occasional nervous passenger, then taking the chase vehicle and following the balloon. When the pilot has located a field for landing, the crew will be informed by radio. The crew must be there before the balloon lands, <u>but every single flight is different in that any change in the wind will mean the crew must adapt to it; this is the main problem since not even the pilot can predict things exactly</u>.

Interviewer: So not anyone can be ground crew?

Patrick Shaw: I'd say that the main skill of ground crew has little to do with the technical aspects of ballooning <u>and more to do with dealing with the public</u>. When the balloon is landing, the crew has to ask the landowner for permission to retrieve the balloon, <u>avoiding any conflict</u> and ensuring we're not disturbing or damaging property. And yes, some tasks do require a little bit of strength, but don't worry, the majority don't.

Interviewer: As a pilot, how do you get on with the ground crew?

Patrick Shaw: Pilots must get on with them. I've never treated any of the crew's questions as if they were silly, not even when I've been asked the same question by the same person over and over again. <u>A new crew member has to understand that every task the crew performs is performed in a certain manner for a reason</u>. When I see <u>somebody ignoring an instruction because they can't see the point of it, that makes me very cross</u>.

Interviewer: Do you take part in balloon competitions?

Patrick Shaw: Oh, yes, they're fun. Balloons don't race in the normal sense of the word. The objective is to get as close as you can to the target, rather than being the first to finish. And it's tough because unlike most other forms of flying, pilots do not have full control over the direction of flight. Competition pilots, though, have become so skilled in using the wind to their advantage that <u>the difference between first place and third or fourth can be just a few centimetres, which leads to some heated arguments</u>.

Interviewer: What makes you such a good pilot, Patrick?

Patrick Shaw: All balloon pilots need a licence to fly. They must have at least thirty-five hours of flight instruction, get basic aviation training and pass a written test. But it's the hours of flying after that that gives you total confidence in your skills. You do things that you wouldn't have dared do when you started out. Like gently brushing the bottom of the basket across the top of a bush or tree so that the occupants can pick up a leaf as a souvenir of the flight.

Interviewer: Wow, sounds great! Patrick, thank you.

Test 3, Paper 4: Listening, Part 1 (page 58)

You will hear people talking in eight different situations. For questions 1–8, choose the best answer (A, B or C).

1
We all knew that in the end Sam, the hero, would win back the love of his girlfriend, Clare. I don't think there was much doubt about that, after all, series like this don't go in for unhappy endings, if they did, they wouldn't attract such large audiences. After weeks of drama and tears, we all wanted to leave the characters on a high note, and that's fair enough. But you'd have thought the scriptwriters would've produced a compelling last episode, to do justice to what was, up to that point, a good series. But because most of the plot lines had resolved themselves the week before, it really wasn't worth watching.

2
People normally request the big names from the DJ, but I've got a huge collection, so there isn't much I can't offer. Sometimes somebody comes up to me and requests a song that makes me say, 'Yeah! That's an awesome track, I'll put that on right now!' Sometimes it's something I don't particularly like, but it doesn't bother me because it's all part of the job, and I don't even mind playing old stuff, because that adds variety. But what I can't stand is when someone requests a track and you have to tell them you've just played it – that does get to me, even if it's a band I really like.

3
This is a collection of paintings from all over the world. There are four large rooms, with paintings from the seventeenth to the twentieth centuries. I wish they'd devoted one room to each century instead of grouping the paintings according to topic. I'd have found it more interesting. They were all landscapes by famous painters – and if you were interested, there was something about the artist and the actual place where they painted. I find that reading things about a painting distracts my attention, but I did buy a book about the exhibition on my way out. There were about one hundred paintings, which is impressive for a small gallery.

4
We've got a vacancy in our sales department and we'd like a young person, ideally somebody just out of college. This job involves face-to-face contact with customers, and there'll be problems to solve for them. We're offering a full training in customer care, and the rest is learnt on the job. All you need is lots of enthusiasm. But, of course, we do need somebody who can produce a report in clear English, and we don't give any training in that. And just in case you're thinking perhaps you need to be good at maths, we have an accounts department that takes care of all that, so it's not an issue.

5
Restaurant Owner: I opened the restaurant two weeks ago, and most days it's quite full. I was interviewed the other day for an article in *Good Eating* magazine, and that'll probably attract even more people!

Interviewer: Well, it may be that your very good website is making people want to come and give you a try. I don't know if you designed it, but it's very attractive indeed.

Restaurant Owner: Actually, it was professionally done, though I'm sure you're right. My wife wasn't very keen on spending the money on it, she reckons satisfied customers tell their friends, and that's enough.

Interviewer: Mmm, she may have a point, of course. You'll have to wait and see.

6
This was partly a holiday and partly a study trip, to see the places we'd studied in our geography lessons. I went with three friends from school, which was great because we organised the whole trip together and got on so well. I'd always travelled with my family, and this experience has been so important in making me realise I can actually do things on my own. I speak good Spanish so I was doing all the talking because neither of my friends know a word of it. But by the end of the trip they'd learnt the basics, and could more or less manage to make themselves understood.

7

There's a lot of talk nowadays about how children should be doing more sport and spending less time in front of the television or computer. Nobody doubts the fact that sport is good for your health, so I didn't feel it was necessary to deal with this in my article. My intention was to raise awareness of a key problem we need to address. We can't just say, 'go out and play a sport' without first investing more on sports venues. We need to look at how other countries deal with this problem, and also at what we can learn from the past.

8

Camping is the best kind of holiday for me. I spend a lot of time planning each trip, so I can definitely give you some good advice. I believe in making sure I'll be warm and comfortable, so I take what some of my friends think is a completely unnecessary amount of clothing, in case it gets cold or wet. Well, it's always worked for me, and I think they're crazy when I see the amount of food they take, which I wouldn't advise you to do, because it's always possible to find things locally. Wherever you're camping – there's always a village not too far away.

Test 3, Paper 4: Listening, Part 2 (page 60)

You will hear a radio programme about the history of roller skating. For questions 9–18, complete the sentences.

In today's programme, I'm going to be talking about roller skating: how the sport started and how it has developed over the years. So who was the first person to come up with the idea of attaching wheels to the feet in order to get about more quickly and easily?

Well, roller skates are not a new invention. In fact, roller skating developed out of the much older activity of ice-skating, which has existed in Scandinavia and other northern countries for centuries. The actual inventor of the first roller skates is not known, but it is generally thought that they originated in Holland in the early 1700s.

Roller skates first arrived in Britain in 1760, when the Belgian clockmaker John Merlin wore some to a formal ball in London. Merlin was known as something of a mad inventor, but he surprised everybody at the ball when he whizzed past them on wheels, playing the violin at the same time. Unfortunately, Merlin did not manage to persuade people that roller skating was a good idea. His skates had no brakes and he ended up crashing into a large mirror. Merlin was quite seriously injured in

the accident and, as a result, roller skating did not immediately become popular in Britain.

In Germany, however, roller skates made a better impression. They were used in a ballet with the name *Winter Pleasures*, which included a scene where the dancers skated on ice. Because they couldn't produce the ice on stage, the organisers decided to use roller skates instead.

After this, the sport gradually became more popular, but it was only thanks to technical advances that it became safer. In 1863, an American named James Plimpton solved the problem of controlling direction when skating by fitting them with rubber springs. His design is widely regarded as the origin of the modern roller skate, although rubber toe brakes, another important safety feature didn't come in until the 1870s.

The late nineteenth century saw the beginnings of events such as speed contests, artistic displays and roller dancing as well as the first team sport on roller skates, roller hockey.

During the first decades of the twentieth century, hundreds of indoor and outdoor roller skating rinks opened, especially in the USA, and the sport became really established as a popular pastime. The first roller skating championships were held in Detroit in 1937.

The real development of the modern roller skate only began in the second half of the twentieth century. From the 1950s onwards, the use of plastics led to improvements in the design and performance of roller skates, and roller disco movies of the 1970s and 1980s increased the popularity of the sport, with roller discos opening in many parts of the world. Meanwhile, the stage musical *Starlight Express,* which features roller skating, ran for seventeen years and was seen by eight million people.

The sport of roller skating has also been gaining a more serious following, especially in southern Europe and South America. The biggest modern change to roller skates came in 1983 with the introduction of in-line skates, also known as rollerblades. Then during the 1990s, new materials, brakes and boot fastenings all combined to make skates both lighter and safer than they had ever been in the past.

So why is roller skating so popular? I went to talk to some fans at a rink in Huddersfield ...

You will hear five different students talking about their first year at university. For questions 19–23, choose from the list (A–F) what each student says. Use the letters only once. There is one extra letter which you do not need to use.

Speaker 1

I decided to study history – I want to be a lecturer one day. When you want to do a degree, say in pharmacy, there's little difference in content between universities, I think. But history at one university can be very different to history at another, so I had to do some research about the three colleges where I might've wanted to study. I'd heard good things about Dundee university, and they all proved correct. I'm from Ireland and I got to study Irish history, plus a focus on the European Union. I've been so busy, I've had no time to enjoy student parties, but that'll come, I'm sure.

Speaker 2

I'd always thought I wanted to study medicine, but the college I wanted to go to only had twenty places and I didn't get a place. That was disappointing and I even thought I might take a year out, but then I had second thoughts about my choice of subject and went for nursing. I'm now at Sheffield Hallam college, which is linked to a variety of hospitals and isn't too far away from home – though far enough for me to be independent. People who'd gone there told me it was really good and the tutors had time for you. The course is brilliant and there's a friendly campus atmosphere.

Speaker 3

I'm studying for a degree in French at Sussex University. It's a part-time course, very few students would want to study part-time for a first degree, of course. Part-time study is mainly for people like me, who have other responsibilities – I work mornings in a school, and I'm keen to keep it that way. I'm learning a lot, though it's been different to what I expected – I thought it was going to be easier! Unlike me, full-time students live in accommodation on the campus, and I hear wonderful stories about the great parties they organise. They say I don't know what I'm missing, but I don't mind, really.

Speaker 4

Psychology was always my choice of degree subject. I studied it at school and soon realised it was what I wanted to do at university. My parents tried hard, but failed, to make me change my mind – they said I was making the wrong choice and that I wouldn't be able to make a living. But I love it. I'm interested in social psychology, how people interact – it's fascinating, and I know I'll be able to find work easily. I'm at Coventry University, living in student accommodation, which is very convenient. Coventry is really student-oriented and the teachers are very friendly. And my brother lives only twenty minutes away, so I see him often.

Speaker 5

I'm studying geography at Swansea University, because I love this area. I came the first day thinking, what if I find out the course isn't what I wanted? But it's amazing, the department is really good and what really does it for me is that it's been brilliant in other ways – pretty much every weekend there's a chance for students to go out. There's a group of us who knew each other from school and we're all starting together. I'm still living at home, but I hope to be able to do some part-time work and rent a small flat with a couple of friends next year.

You will hear an interview with the film actor Mikey Standish. For questions 24–30, choose the best answer (A, B or C).

Interviewer: With us today is the actor Mikey Standish. Mikey, with your career on the up, do you want to be the next Leonardo DiCaprio?

Mikey Standish: I don't really try to be anyone else. I know that's what is said about me, and it upsets me, because I'm just trying to experience as many different types and styles of acting as I can. So it's not fair. I've managed to play a wide range of roles. The cinema industry usually wants to see you doing the same thing all the time, but I prefer to stretch myself.

Interviewer: In your latest film, *The Waterfall*, you play Simon, a young man very much like yourself.

Mikey Standish: Yeah, um, I thought it was going to be easy, because it's closer to me. I'd been in full-time education for twenty years, like Simon has. Simon's middle class, I'm middle class, etc, etc. So I understood where the guy was coming from. But actually, that made it kind of frightening because if you're not careful there's no character to hide behind, if you know what I mean. But doing it has certainly made me into a better actor.

Interviewer: Are there any character types that you would prefer not to play?

Mikey Standish: Yeah. I once played this man who was a real waste of time. We've seen that so often, the unworthy, totally uninteresting person who then turns out to have the answer to everything, I want no part in that. I don't mind continuing to play the romantic lead, but the character must develop in a way that's believable.

Interviewer: How old were you when you decided that acting was something that you wanted to do?

Mikey Standish: I applied for drama college before I decided that acting was what I wanted to do for the rest of my life. I was offered a film when I was sixteen and I did it. I got that part just out of the blue, with a French director, and then I didn't act for two years. I worked in a bakery and tried to get on at school, but I wasn't doing too well. So it was either leave school and stay in the bakery, which was out of the question, really, or try drama school because I'd done this one film and I might get in.

Interviewer: And what would you tell the kids who are interested or thinking about acting as a career?

Mikey Standish: I think drama school is the best thing. It's the environment where you realise whether you want to do it or not. You're competitive all the time in the real world, and this competitive element can make you carry on, though the job might be something you're not suited to, or something that you maybe don't even like. But the competition can keep you going and that's not good, it's not healthy.

Interviewer: How do you cope with being a celebrity?

Mikey Standish: I'm lucky, I've been doing this work for seven years now, so it's not, like, happened overnight. Over the last few years, I've been getting recognised on the street more and more often as the press coverage has increased, but I can handle it OK. Had it been, like, bang! suddenly you're a star and your life's not your own any more, who knows, I might not have coped so well.

Interviewer: So what's your next movie?

Mikey Standish: I'll do something I have always wanted to do, which is a sci-fi movie. It's not starting till next year, and I've had some calls from a director asking if I could fit in another movie in the meantime. It was a very tempting offer, which would've involved me in actually producing the script as well. But the truth is that I've done five films without much of a break, so I'm definitely in need of a bit of time off. As from tomorrow actually.

Interviewer: Right. Mikey Standish, thank you and I hope you enjoy your break.

You will hear people talking in eight different situations. For questions 1–8, choose the best answer (A, B or C).

1
Schools no longer have queues of kids saying they want to join the choir. It never used to be difficult to get children involved as all primary school children used to learn to sing in class. Unfortunately this practice has declined in recent years, and I'm sure most parents would agree with me about the reason for this. Fewer of today's teachers feel confident to lead the singing, let alone accompany it on a keyboard. If children reach adolescence without having learnt to sing with others with enjoyment and without embarrassment, there's little chance of them ever taking it up.

2
M: So, you've taken to going to evening classes!

F: Yes, I thought January was the perfect time to try something new; change things I wasn't happy with. The course in digital photography sounded ideal because it's so different from my coursework at college, which was overloading me and making me feel anxious.

M: Right.

F: I didn't know then that it would actually look good on my CV and give me an extra thirty credits on top of my degree, which isn't bad for a few hours' work a week. I might even find that when I go on holiday with my friends, I'll be entrusted with taking the photos!

3
F: Well, I reckon Café Promo's doing well. It's the perfect place to stop for a coffee and a bite to eat when you're out in town.
M: Yes, they're really making an effort to offer something a little bit different. They obviously want to stand out from the more predictable coffee chains. And they do great baguettes and sandwiches with really generous fillings.

F: Rather too generous for my liking, but good value I guess. People want something a bit out of the ordinary, and they've certainly succeeded in doing that. Now they need to pay more attention to training their staff, but I think that'll come.

M: It may do.

4

He made it sound so adventurous and … liberating when he said: 'It's the total freedom of it, escaping the world, leaving civilization behind. It's like exploring outer space.' After that I changed my mind about caving. What had previously seemed a rather puzzling, even unappealing, pastime became a passion thanks to the enthusiasm of this instructor. I was joining a group of other college students, and together with a TV journalist and camera crew we were off to discover the realities of life underground. I hoped that I wouldn't make a fool of myself on television; I was more frightened of that than I was of the actual physical and mental challenges ahead of me.

5

I think on the whole the interview went rather well. They put me at ease straight away. Mr Grant started off by talking about the company, and I found those five minutes really useful to collect myself. Then he asked me a number of questions and I was glad for the opportunity to talk about the various experiences I've had. However, another time I'd go along with specific examples of my achievements to hand. When one of them asked the first question I thought: 'Gosh, I can't think of a time I've done that.' I think the interview was about my qualifications, but also about being the right fit for the company.

6

I've just finished my first year and I have some good things to say about the course. I thought it would be all girls on it, but I was surprised to see how many guys there are. I've gained a basic knowledge of the language – Spanish grammar isn't easy, I can tell you. I've been told it all gets more intense from September. I was hoping I'd be thrown in at the deep end, that I'd be fluent by the end of the year. It's disappointing. That won't happen now. Most of my classmates are doing other languages as well, and they're happy with this pace.

7

My whole life has been talking about food really, though I've never been tempted to write about it. Me and my wife, at dinner we'll sit, eat and talk about where we're going to source a new product from. I get excited about how we present food on the shelves. Sometimes I even get excited about the boxes food comes in or the way the grower has presented it. I like to provide the local restaurants with food that is fresh, and to support local farmers and small growers. I've been interviewed for radio and television twice, so I'm really concerned I might become a celebrity one of these days!

8

I moved here with my wife and children three months ago, from the city, we wanted a quieter life. But a week after the move I found myself wanting to go back to the place we'd left, thinking, that's it, I'm too old for this, the friends I've got won't bother to come this far to see me. It lasted a few days, and I'm afraid it worried my wife a lot – she'd keep telling me how nice the people next door were, how they'd given us this lovely bunch of flowers, how the kids had already made some friends. She didn't understand it wasn't about that at all.

Test 4, Paper 4: Listening, Part 2 (page 80)

You will hear a radio programme about a day in the life of a television researcher. For questions 9–18, complete the sentences.

Hi. My name's Rita Lewis and I've come along today to tell you about my work. I'm a researcher on a television programme and I'm going to tell you about a typical working day in my job. Well, quite an exciting day actually.

But first of all, I should explain that I work on a wildlife programme. I've always been interested in the sciences and animals in particular, and I did my first degree in biology before going on to specialise in zoology in my second degree. My degree subjects are invaluable in my job as they help me to plan things like deciding which animals to film, where to find them and how to approach them. But I also did a post-graduate course in what's known as media studies that prepared me specifically for the television work, and it was the combination of the two things that really got me the job.

The job has taken me to a variety of countries including South Africa and Australia, but the day I'm going to tell you about was last winter, when I was in Costa Rica. I was in the jungle doing some filming for the programme.

I woke up at five-thirty in my room at the Corcovado National Park research centre. Before setting off we had to pack up our filming gear, which weighs fifty kilos, and head out to the first location. Fortunately there are twelve of us in the team, including three cameramen and a local guide. So we could share the load between us.

For this particular TV series the presenter, who's called Jamie, had to complete a variety of difficult wildlife challenges. You know the sort of thing, communicating with wild monkeys, eating insects, etc. Anyway, that morning he had to photograph a poisonous type of frog, and that meant getting pretty close. The animals are not that hard to find, and fortunately our guide found one very quickly. I had to hold it very carefully, though, while Jamie got his camera ready. For me this is the best part of the job, when I get to interact with the animals.

Our first location was on top of a thirty-metre high waterfall. First of all we wanted to film Jamie abseiling over the edge. Next we needed to get a shot of the same action from below. We can't risk sending the camera down on ropes, so we have to walk for an hour-and-a-half hike through heavy jungle to the pools beneath.

By the time we'd done that it was lunchtime. Some of the crew tucked into chicken legs and cheese sandwiches, but I'd got tuna in mine, which was fine for me. I ate them on a completely empty, beautiful beach, and they tasted like the best sandwiches ever.

After lunch, the team relaxed for the afternoon, before the evening's filming. Jamie's next challenge was to cross a river where crocodiles live. The river is near the sea, so we had to wait for the right tides. You need to use a torch to spot the crocodiles' red eyes glowing in the dark and make sure they're not too close before you set out across the river.

We found a safe place to film and set up our lights. We were using what we call a 'Sun Gun' light, which is used to film in large areas at night. Jamie was just about to step into the water when the light went out. Fortunately we had a smaller standby light, so we taped that onto the camera. We shone the new light over where Jamie was about to step. There, right in front of him was a 3-metre-long crocodile. It must have come up from under the water while we were changing our equipment. That was close.

We moved upstream where the water was lower. Jamie finally crossed, but when you see the programme, you'll see he looks genuinely scared on screen, which is unusual for him as he's usually really calm and relaxed on camera, whatever he's doing. So it was an exciting day. For me, getting out in the wild is the best part of the job.

Test 4, Paper 4: Listening, Part 3 (page 81)

You will hear five different craft workers giving advice to people who want to start a home-based business to sell the things they make. For questions 19–23, choose from the list (A–F) what advice each speaker gives. Use the letters only once. There is one extra letter which you do not need to use.

Speaker 1
Most people who are interested in starting craft businesses enjoy making or doing something, whether it's making dolls, candles, or even cooking. But it's not as easy as it might seem. Some think a good website and a few ads in the papers are all they need for their business to take off and provide a regular income, but there's much more to it than that. I make silver jewellery, and you'll find my style has changed over time, because I've kept doing research into the latest techniques. There's nothing worse than thinking you know it all. However much you advertise, your business will slow down.

Speaker 2
There's such a demand for handmade goods, because people are looking for the personal touch. One day I had the idea of covering some jars and bottles with cloth, then putting a thin coat of plaster on, and painting designs on the surface. I sold them so quickly that I decided to start a business. There were bottles all over my house, in different stages of development, and I wished I'd given more thought to setting up an area where I'd do the work. I lost time and money because I ended up getting in such a mess. So beginners, take notice! I also sell online now, but most of my sales are from word-of-mouth recommendations.

Speaker 3
Doing something you like to do and getting paid for it is great, and it doesn't have to be scary. By the time you actually start selling things, though, it's essential to have a rough bookkeeping system in place and to have worked out the profits you expect and deducted your expenditure and possible losses. I started my own craft business two years ago – making baskets, filling them with things like fruit and nuts, and decorating them with silk flowers. I wrapped them as gifts and sold them to friends at first, but now I have lots of orders. I'm even thinking of employing a couple of people.

Speaker 4
When you're ready to launch your business, it pays to think carefully about how your prospective customers will hear about you. There's little point in taking out ads in the national papers at this stage, but it may well pay to invest in a colourful brochure and posters, which can be left in shops in the area. That's how I started my business, which is designing and making greeting cards. Mind you, friends and acquaintances gave me contradictory advice, and I ended up paying someone to design a website for me when I wasn't ready for it. Anyway, my business is thriving and now takes up five rooms in my house!

Speaker 5

I started making lampshades, and it just went from hobby to career. My home no longer offers enough space, so I may rent some extra rooms from a friend. It was good to start small, though, I wouldn't have been able to cope with lots of work then. I really knew nothing about marketing, and if you're like me, don't worry; if your products sell, it'll sort itself out. I owe part of my success to my brother who designed an amazing website for me, which attracted lots of buyers. It does mean you need to organise a way to post things securely, but it's all worthwhile doing.

Test 4, Paper 4: Listening, Part 4 (page 82)

You will hear an interview with Monica Darcey, who has written a bestselling book about gardening. For questions 24–30, choose the best answer (A, B or C).

Interviewer: Monica, welcome to the programme. Your book *Make your garden unique* has been a great success. But why would people want to buy a book about gardening instead of just buying some plants and putting them in the ground?

Monica Darcey: Hello! Well, yes, I think that's what most people do when they move into a place, there's often little time to think. Lots of readers have written to me saying that's what they'd done, gone to a garden centre, spent a lot of money on seeds and plants, with not very good results. In fact I think people with that sort of experience make up the majority of my readers!

Interviewer: So, how did your interest in gardening start? Were your parents keen gardeners?

Monica Darcey: Well, people imagine I must come from a family of gardeners. In fact, my parents would have much rather seen me developing an interest in sport, as they were both water sports teachers. But I was forever catching colds and that put me off. Seeing me spending hours in the garden, showing little interest in the world outside plants was a cause for concern rather than pride for them though.

Interviewer: And how did you go from gardener to writer?

Monica Darcey: Well, I did win a short-story prize at school, and enjoyed writing essays at college, but I had no real passion for writing then. I was making a good living looking after gardens. Then one day I was working in a nature reserve and I had to write about my day at work for an environmental project. It gave me such a feeling of achievement that when I saw an advert for a gardening journalist on a magazine, I applied, thinking I could do it in my spare time when I wasn't gardening.

Interviewer: And you got the job?

Monica Darcey: I did, but after a while they made me an editor, which was a kind of promotion, but editors tend to find themselves doing everything but writing, and I'm happiest when being creative, so I decided it was time for a change. My bosses weren't very happy about it, I must say. So I went back to working all hours planting trees and flowers.

Interviewer: And that's when you starting writing your book, is that right?

Monica Darcey: Yes, and I've never looked back, really. I'm now writing my second book, about gardens around the world.

Interviewer: So, what makes your gardening books so special for readers?

Monica Darcey: It takes years of experience to learn to write attractively. It must flow perfectly when you read it, as if it had required no effort at all. But to answer your question, I suppose it's the fact that I'm not merely providing information, because that would make a jolly dull piece of writing – I don't assume everyone's fascinated by gardening, and I include some interviews, the kind of personal experience that may amuse the reader. Of course the information is all correct, and well researched, but that has to be the case with any serious writer.

Interviewer: Do you choose the photographs for your books?

Monica Darcey: I do. The quality of photography is excellent now of course. It's been a fantastic development in that it's brought many more people into gardening. Magazines and books devote a lot of space to photography, and quite rightly. But the pictures often show how things might be, rather than how they are, that's my only criticism. The writing's still the important part though, readers don't just buy beautiful pictures.

Interviewer: Finally, we've heard you've been asked to take part in a TV programme.

Monica Darcey: I have, and I'm still thinking about it. The idea is that I'd interview people who've designed some of the most amazing gardens in Europe – it would get me away from my writing routine which does get a bit too much at times, and it would give me plenty of ideas. It's also true that such a programme can make you into a kind of celebrity, and I'm not sure I'm ready for that, you know, you start being recognised in the street. Although my publisher says that that's something I should be really happy about!

You will hear people talking in eight different situations. For questions 1–8, choose the best answer (A, B or C).

1

And now the weather for the weekend. I'm afraid it's not good news for sports enthusiasts. After a cloudy and rather windy Saturday morning, there's a risk of showers in the afternoon, which will turn heavier and stay with us for the whole of Sunday. The temperatures will remain stable but low for this time of year, at no more than 10 degrees centigrade on Saturday, rising slightly on Sunday afternoon. There will be moderate south-west winds throughout the weekend, but they should die down by Sunday evening. That's the weather for the weekend. I'm Mark Schapiro at the Midlands Weather Centre.

2

I'm not sure what I've done to my arm. This muscle really hurts and I can't do the simplest of things, not even the washing-up at home! It might have happened at the office when I tried to lift some heavy boxes, but, more likely, I may have overdone things with the weights. Everyone seems so fit here, but of course I've only been doing regular exercise for a couple of months. I'd really appreciate it if you could change my workout programme to make it a bit lighter. It's such a busy time at work I can't risk having to miss a day again.

3

Do you find it difficult to follow a recipe in a cookery book? Sam Gordon, the famous cook and writer, will teach you how to cook even if you've never as much as fried an egg. He'll guide you through basic preparation techniques which you'll be able to follow in your own kitchen, step by step, and if you get into trouble, you'll be able to phone the studio live. Sam says he can guarantee that you'll be so enthusiastic about cooking after his lessons that he'll have you dashing out to the nearest book store to buy his recipe collection!

4

We've been talking about Jane's problems all morning, and I don't think it helps in the least. It doesn't help Jane, or you, or me. In fact, I find this rather painful, because it just proves that something should've been done about it years ago. It would've been possible to help her then, but I chose to do nothing. I think I was feeling tired, fed up with the whole situation, which was the same, day after day after day. Anyway, I think you should try and relax and find yourself an activity that'll take your mind off the problem.

5

When you buy a fashion magazine, do you ask yourself why you see nothing but photos of models wearing the sort of clothes that you'll never be able to afford? If what you want is to wear that look that'll turn people's heads in the street and make you look like a model on the catwalk, without paying the earth, then look no further than *Fashion Crazy*. This is a great weekly: inspiring fashion and an expert look at the latest designer collections – what to wear and what fashion disasters to avoid at any cost!

6

I'm in two minds about selling my flat. I'll be working at home from next month and there's no way I can fit a desk and all my files in here. And I could choose to live anywhere, really – distance from the office will no longer be an issue. But it's so gorgeous in summer when it's hot – with the windows open you can look out over the rooftops all around you. And you'd think it would be noisy, with all the traffic down below, but as soon as you close the windows you're in a different world, maybe because it's on the fourth floor.

7

The Society for the Protection of Forest Wildlife will be holding its monthly meeting in the Town Hall on Saturday. Harry Foster, the director, will be giving a presentation on the latest achievements of the Society in the preservation of endangered bird species. This is a chance not just for members of the Society but for the general public to hear how the money is being spent. To do its work, the Society relies on financial contributions from the government and also on the generous support of the public who have helped to plant hundreds of new trees to improve the forest habitat.

8

F: Why don't you play a proper game in the open air instead of computer games?

M: You don't understand. I never enjoyed sport as a kid, I found games awfully stressful. I always knew I was going to lose – I wasn't a very competitive type. Instead, with computer games I know I can win if I put my mind to it, or I can always go back and find out why I lost. Computer games are having this amazing effect on me, and they've even helped in my attitude to work. I can face up to stressful situations in a way I couldn't in the past.

Test 5, Paper 4: Listening, Part 2 (page 100)

You will hear a radio programme about a bird called a peacock. For questions 9–18, complete the sentences.

In this evening's talk I'm going to be telling you about the peacock, which is one of the world's most spectacular birds and a great favourite in zoos and tourist attractions in many countries. The peacock is best known for its tail, which is huge and brightly coloured and, sort of, stands up behind it. People say that it looks like a fan. When the bird opens and closes this tail, it's a wonderful sight.

There are two main types of peacock, the blue and the green. The green peacock lives in Southeast Asia, in countries such as Thailand, Malaysia and Indonesia, whereas the blue peacock originally comes from India. And it's the blue peacock that you are more likely to see in other parts of the world, because it is better able to live in different climates than its green cousin. And it has been kept by humans for many centuries.

In ancient cultures, blue peacocks were kept both because they looked nice and also because they were good to eat. The Ancient Romans certainly had them two thousand years ago, and there is evidence of them in Ancient Egypt three thousand years ago. But it is thought that the first culture to keep the birds were the Mesopotamians, who lived four thousand years ago.

Now, as I said earlier, the blue peacock is spectacular to look at. The bird has a long thin neck and a very small head on a big body and looks a bit like a turkey. It's only when it opens its tail that you realise how beautiful it is. The tail, which stands up behind the bird, grows to a length of over two hundred centimetres and is a wonderful shiny blue-green colour. This tail is covered with large egg-shaped spots which are called 'eyes'. It makes a wonderful pattern and in the sunlight the colours are magnificent, the blues, greens and blacks turning to purple, black and gold.

Unfortunately, it is only the male bird that has this tail because the purpose of all this wonderful display is to attract a mate. The female bird, which is actually called the peahen, is brown and rather dull looking compared to her multicoloured mate. The male walks up and down displaying his tail to impress the female bird. It's such a famous sight that we even find reference to it in different languages. In English,

for example, we have the expression 'as proud as a peacock' to describe men who take a lot of trouble over their appearance.

In the wild, the peacock's natural habitat is the forest, where they live in small family groups. They like to live near water in hilly jungle areas. Although they can fly quite well, they cannot go very fast and they usually only fly for short distances, usually to escape from danger. When danger approaches, they warn each other by making loud shrieking noises. Although they spend most of their time on the ground, peacocks usually sleep in trees. They move into the lower branches in the late afternoon and then gradually move higher up as night falls.

One of the best places in the world to see different types of peacocks is called Peacock Paradise and it is located in Melaka in Malaysia. There you can see both types of bird, and there's also a visitor centre which provides lots of information about peacocks and other similar birds. There's even a pool full of crocodiles to watch if you need a change from birds! If you get the chance to go, it's certainly worth a visit.

Test 5, Paper 4: Listening, Part 3 (page 101)

You will hear five different writers talking about their first novels. For questions 19–23, choose from the list (A–F) what each writer says. Use the letters only once. There is one extra letter which you do not need to use.

Speaker 1
I'd never done any writing before, though I was a keen reader. This novel was inspired by my own childhood experiences – I got to meet a lot of people as a child because my parents owned a large, successful restaurant. I don't think I could've written it if I hadn't decided to take a degree in creative writing a few years ago, though. It was a way of being serious about writing and it gave me a lot of confidence. I began work on the novel halfway through the second year, and completed it after graduating. It was very, very hard work, but it's all really been worthwhile.

Speaker 2
I'm only twenty-two years old, and I've been writing since I was thirteen – mainly short stories which were published in teen magazines. When I started writing a novel I realised the way I'd written so far wasn't so good really, not for real fiction. So I knew I had to look at my favourite writers – you learn a lot by seeing how they do what they do. I knew very well what I wanted to write about, though. I get bored with books where everyone is a bit like someone you

know. I wanted to write about people who only exist in fiction. That's what readers find attractive.

Speaker 3
My novel began life as a blog on my website. Within a week of starting it, <u>I'd been offered a book deal by a publisher. I remember sitting and looking at this offer on my computer screen</u>. The sum was several times bigger than my annual librarian's salary and I thought there must've been some mistake. The novel is a fictional version of my blog, and it centres on a university librarian, his partner and their sons. Writing it wasn't particularly hard because basically I was being asked to keep to the same style. And I'm now adapting it for the screen. I'd always wanted a job that I could really enjoy.

Speaker 4
I used to watch a lot of TV, and I admit that the inspiration for my novel came from the dramas I watched, or rather from my disappointment at how unrealistic and far-fetched they were. It was very rarely that any of them attempted to get under the skin of the characters. <u>So that's what I aimed to do – tell it like it was.</u> It wasn't easy, and when people say how wonderful it must be to be recognised in the street and to be asked to sign autographs, I tell them about the long hours in front of the computer, and about forgetting what it means to have a free weekend.

Speaker 5
<u>I used to be a journalist</u> on a national paper and I began work on my novel in 2001. It's a historical novel and I spent months researching the history of the period – it's set in India in the 1920s. I then spent two years writing it. <u>Journalism wasn't a bad place to acquire useful skills.</u> It taught me to be clear and edit myself, not to write too much. My parents couldn't believe it when they heard my name on the news. I hadn't told them anything because they never thought very highly of anything I'd written previously, and I didn't want to start having any doubts myself.

Test 5, Paper 4: Listening, Part 4 (page 102)

You will hear an interview with a man called David Shaw, who is a professional ceramicist, making pottery objects out of clay. For questions 24–30, choose the best answer (A, B or C).

Interviewer: David, a career in ceramics seems so attractive. Is that a realistic picture?

David Shaw: Well, for some it's just a job, for others it's a love affair. But in all cases it's crucial you do things at the right stage, <u>nothing can be rushed, if you're the sort of person who can't wait, then this</u> <u>isn't for you!</u> I start by getting all the air bubbles out of the clay. Next, I 'throw' the clay – that's the word we use – I shape it on a wheel, before leaving it to harden. When it's fully dry, I fire it in a kiln at a high temperature, then glaze it, before firing it again. It's physical work – there's lots of slapping the clay and putting pressure on it. You feel tired by the end of the day, but you shouldn't let that put you off.

Interviewer: And it takes time to become a really good artist.

David Shaw: You've got to be determined. I was apprenticed for over two years to another potter, and very soon I was making the sort of shapes that have become a distinctive feature of my pieces. It was relatively easy for me to find my own voice. Not so with the financial side of it, though. That was a steep learning curve and <u>for years I was barely making enough to survive</u>, even though I was putting in long days.

Interviewer: So what's the best part of your job?
David Shaw: <u>I like the way that you don't know exactly what's going to come out of the kiln</u>, because the firing process affects each piece differently. There are other pleasures, but nothing equals that feeling. I still love seeing the finished pots; that I've achieved something tangible. It's also nice to hear people's positive responses. People tell me that they use my cups and dishes every day.

Interviewer: And the most difficult?

David Shaw: Well, I have to do everything – all the paperwork for example. It's not hard work in itself, don't get me wrong, in fact, at times it provides a welcome break from making pots, but it eats up valuable time. If I don't plan my days very carefully, things don't get done because <u>I also need to look at new projects, come up with fresh initiatives, and that's the toughest part of the job</u>. But I'm always keen to fulfil whatever I promise a client – I hate to keep people waiting.

Interviewer: Recently you've been very successful. Why do you think that is?

David Shaw: Yes, I've just designed a dinner service for a famous shop, and I must say it's rare for a potter to do that. It so happened that they were looking for a dinner service in the classical style I do, and <u>I think I was in the right place at the right time</u>. Most potters work on their own, and their money comes from exhibitions. They mostly work extremely hard. Some also teach.

Interviewer: Have you ever considered teaching?

David Shaw: Mmmm … I have, and recently I had a very tempting offer, from one of the best art colleges in this area. They wanted me to teach one morning a week, a special ceramics workshop. It was just a few hours, and it would have given me a different experience. I declined the offer because, yes, I have the knowledge and experience, but I have no teaching qualification. The college principal said I'd pick it up easily enough, but I wasn't convinced.

Interviewer: So, finally, what would you say to a young person who wants a career in ceramics?

David Shaw: Don't believe people who tell you you can do it all yourself. You could go to art school and do a degree in ceramics, but there are also night classes and adult education courses. If you decide you want to do it, focus on it and don't let yourself lose direction. The physical skills develop through practice – you've got to stick with it. You learn to attune your visual sense so you can look at the curves of an object and see what looks good and what doesn't, until you can develop your own style. Have self-belief and be proud of your work.

Interviewer: David, many thanks.

Test 6, Paper 4: Listening, Part 1 (page 118)

You will hear people talking in eight different situations. For questions 1–8, choose the best answer (A, B or C).

1
People think working for a tourist company's a glamorous job, which may well be true if what you do is travel to dreamlike resorts in search of the ideal beach holiday for your clients. That's what one of my colleagues does – she comes back with scores of great photos and that's where I come in, to decide which of them will create the greatest impact in the company's publicity material. But, would you believe it, she complains it's not really a holiday for her! I'd agree if a tour guide said that, the poor guys definitely have no time for anything except dealing with difficult tourists.

2
F: So did you enjoy the film last night?

M: I would've done, if it hadn't been for that couple behind me who seemed to be providing a running commentary. It was barely a whisper, but I could still hear every word. I was sitting on the aisle, as usual, because in other seats there's not enough legroom for me as I'm so tall, but I would've gladly moved somewhere else, if only there'd been an empty seat. But the place was packed, so that wasn't an option.

F: I know what you mean, I know the film well – it's got superb dialogue and you wouldn't want to miss a single word.

3
I volunteered myself to run the marathon. I was at a party and the director of a charity was talking about marathon running, and I said, 'I've always wanted to run the marathon!' and then it was out there, and it was such a lie. I didn't do any sport at school, I used to say I wasn't allowed to run. I left the party thinking, he'll forget all about it. But then he wrote to me and I thought 'I can't back out now.' So I got myself a personal trainer, hit the gym five times a week and ran the marathon in five hours and 13 minutes.

4
It tells the time, maps the stars and calculates the height of buildings. No, it's not the latest James Bond gadget, but a scientific tool from the fourteenth century. It was the pocket calculator of its age and has been acquired by an anonymous collector for a world record of £138,000. This is an extremely rare piece, and there are only seven others in the world. It's made of brass and it had lain hidden under a floor until three years ago when it was discovered during building works. It is thought that the previous owner may have been trying to keep it safe from burglars.

5
I'm all in favour of the latest government policy to invest in facilities for young people, and I'm really pleased that the tax we pay should be used in that way. What I don't understand is this local opposition to having an Internet café, from people who argue that most students have broadband and a laptop, which is just wishful thinking. There are computers in the library, I know, but are they available in the evening? Of course not, and there's no point in extending opening hours – young people want a relaxing environment in the evening, away from books and school.

6
I find theatre directing thrilling. It's also the hardest thing you can do, which is why I wanted to do it. There are very few women running theatres, though we're no less qualified than men. But I do wonder how they combine a career in theatre with motherhood. The two are not really compatible with the late hours, but more and more women just rise to the challenge, which is something I felt unable

to do, as much as I wanted the job. I wouldn't have minded giving up the part-time work I'm doing at the moment, but, who knows, there may be other opportunities later on.

7

I run what I call 'laughter workshops'. The gift of humour is part of the natural apparatus human beings are born with. But my work is about learning to be less fearful of life's experiences because we know we can deal with anything. When I was young I suffered horribly from other children laughing at me, then I started to create that effect deliberately. And now I'm helping others in this way. I start with improvisation exercises to help people introduce themselves to the group. One thing that gets people relaxed and laughing is when I ask them to dance as badly as they can! Everybody can do that.

8

The first thing I noticed about the aeroplane was how small it was. I'm not a particularly nervous flyer but this made me a little apprehensive. I was in safe hands, though. I held my breath while my instructor got us into the air. After a short demonstration of the controls, and a reassuring 'you're not going to be expected to do anything complicated' from my instructor, I was allowed to try them myself. I whipped through the tops of clouds and began to turn the plane about. The vast number of instruments seemed intimidating, but it turned out only one or two are necessary at any one time.

Test 6, Paper 4: Listening, Part 2 (page 120)

You will hear an interview with a man called Daren Howarth, who works as a carbon coach. For questions 9–18, complete the sentences.

Interviewer: Tonight my guest is Daren Howarth who works as a carbon coach. What exactly does that mean Daren?

Daren Howarth: Well, most people know about global warming and would like to do something to reduce the amount of carbon they send out into the atmosphere, but they don't always know the best way of doing this. What I do as a carbon coach is give them advice about how to achieve environmentally friendly living. I'm now a full-time consultant, and my clients include both companies and private individuals.

Interviewer: What made you decide to become a carbon coach?

Daren Howarth: Well it all started about fifteen years ago. I'd always been interested in energy-saving and the environment and I trained as an ecologist. At that time, people were talking about very technical things like greenhouse gas emissions, then someone came up with the term 'carbon footprint', which is much easier for people to understand.

Interviewer: And you can tell ordinary families what their carbon footprint is, can't you?

Daren Howarth: That's right. I work out how much carbon dioxide the family's generated over a year; firstly by studying their bills, then finding out how much waste they produce, how much they use the car, and so on. Adding together all these figures, I calculate their total carbon footprint in tonnes of carbon dioxide. Then I take a look around their home and suggest ways of reducing their carbon footprint.

Interviewer: How do you work out how much carbon each machine around the house emits?

Daren Howarth: By switching off all the things that use electricity, then turning each one on one at a time, you can see the amount of energy each one uses. I use something known as a 'carbon meter' which measures the amount of electricity being used in the house at any one time. It also shows how much carbon dioxide this represents.

Interviewer: What's the least energy efficient thing you've seen in homes?

Daren Howarth: I go into so many places where I look in the roof and there's no insulation, so there's nothing stopping all the heat just going straight out into the outside air. Insulation massively reduces your carbon footprint; it's cheap and the government will help with the cost of it.

Interviewer: So is that the worst thing?

Daren Howarth: Well, central heating systems can be very inefficient and people use things like electric knives and mixers which are unnecessary, but the thing I really can't stand is when people are still using old-fashioned light bulbs. People can't resist them because they're so cheap, but up to ninety percent of the energy they produce is lost as heat. If you have one, put it in a box and smash it up, so no one else can use it.

Interviewer: What other type of clients do you have?

Daren Howarth: We work with both individuals and businesses – and even some celebrities, such as the band *Supergrass*. For one of their albums about three years ago, the band decided <u>to minimise their carbon footprint at their concerts</u> and then also cut the amount of carbon produced when making a CD. The carbon footprint for a disc is just a few grams, but a big band like *Supergrass* will produce thousands of copies, which means several tonnes of carbon.

Interviewer: And what are your plans for the future?

Daren Howarth: I'm working hard on introducing a really green type of home in this country <u>known as an Earthship</u>. It's a building that creates its own energy, heats and cools itself, collects its own water and deals with its own waste. It's also built from recycled materials. It doesn't need electricity or gas for heating, as it captures and stores energy <u>by using wind power, and solar panels</u> on the roof charge up batteries which provide power.

Interviewer: Any disadavantages?

Daren Howarth: You have to change your lifestyle and keep an eye on changes in the weather. There are thousands of examples around the world and <u>there's a handbook on sale</u> that explains everything about it – you'll find the details on my website – and it's something you can do for yourself – you don't have to employ someone to do the work for you.

Interviewer: Well Daren thanks for telling us about carbon footprints and how we can all …

Test 6, Paper 4: Listening, Part 3 (page 121)

You will hear five different people talking about the sport of hill walking. For questions 19–23, choose from the list (A–F) the reason why each person took up the sport. Use the letters only once. There is one extra letter which you do not need to use.

Speaker 1
I was very unfit but determined to do some hill walking. The first time I went though, my companions almost gave up on me. They had to keep stopping while I caught my breath or rested aching muscles – not surprising, really, as I'd never been one for sports or trips to the gym. So the walk was no fun for them, even less so for me. But as I couldn't face the thought of going alone, <u>I knew I had to get myself fit enough to be accepted as a full member of the group</u>. I decided hill walking would be my road to fitness, and by persevering, I got there.

Speaker 2
I'm a very fit person because I've been going to the gym and doing different sports for years. The problem was that, being a very competitive person, I found it difficult to really relax. After reading interviews with

hill walkers, I was convinced that this sport would give me <u>a sense of achievement without the pressure: that it was something I'd actually enjoy doing</u>. It wasn't easy knowing where to start, though. Fortunately, I met an experienced walker who'd climbed the highest hills in Scotland. He gave me some tips, and then I just went for it, on my own, because I don't believe in walking in groups.

Speaker 3
For me, hill walking's been a real challenge. When I first started, I often wanted to turn back when I was only halfway up a hill. I would ask myself: 'Why am I doing this?' But I knew the answer really. <u>I'd failed spectacularly when I'd tried to get fit playing tennis or swimming</u>, maybe because I wasn't making enough of an effort, but I couldn't see the point. With hill walking, I could feel it was strengthening my legs and the aerobic exercise was just wonderful. An unexpected bonus was making so many friends because you immediately have something in common with people you meet on the hill.

Speaker 4
I used to have a personal trainer, who believed conventional fitness tests were rubbish. He always said: 'All you need to know is how fit you feel now, and how fit you need to be to achieve your own goals.' He trained me in the gym, which improved my muscle tone and my strength in general, <u>but my goal was to one day climb Kilimanjaro, which is at a really high altitude</u>. But to have a chance of reaching the summit, I clearly needed to make a start by climbing some smaller hills! My trainer said I shouldn't give up the gym, but you can't do everything, can you?

Speaker 5
I quite enjoy the hills these days, though it's still a real physical effort, but I think that's the case for lots of people. When I get to the top, though, I'm totally buzzing with what I've achieved. I played football regularly until I was twenty, <u>then I discovered there was something wrong with one of my knees, and I was advised to try hill walking, which was supposed to strengthen it</u>. I liked it so much that I've never looked back, though my knee is absolutely fine now. I'm now trying to organise a hill-walking group because the sport's so much more fun when you can share it.

Test 6, Paper 4: Listening, Part 4 (page 122)

You will hear an interview with a woman called Jennie Thorpe, who is a trapeze artist in a circus. For questions 24–30, choose the best answer (A, B or C).

Interviewer: Jennie, welcome to the programme. A job in a circus, on the flying trapeze, sounds like a dream. How did you become a trapeze artist?

Jennie Thorpe: I'd say first of all that it's not that magical – it's work. You have to work extremely hard, but if you have the physical capacity and talent, it's not that difficult. I did gymnastics and ballet as a child before joining a youth circus at fourteen. I'd been in a number of ballet shows so I felt confident. Then I studied at a circus school for three years, and as part of the training I did a number of performances there. The manager of the circus I now work for saw me in one of them and offered me a job. But I know that they also recruit acrobats from gymnastic competitions.

Interviewer: Do you have to practise every day?

Jennie Thorpe: I perform at night, so I like to sleep in, then practise on stage for forty-five minutes. I perform my trapeze act once or twice a day, nine or ten times every week. Before each show, I put on my make-up and sparkly costume, and warm up for half-an-hour, doing handstands and abdominal push-ups. I have to do a lot of strength and flexibility exercises. After the show, I practise again for at least another half-an-hour. That's when my muscles are warmest, so I can push my body even harder.

Interviewer: Is a trapeze artist job well-paid, is it enough to live on comfortably?

Jennie Thorpe: We get paid per show, and the amount depends on how you've negotiated your contract, but it's usually very good. I've only met two trapeze artists in their late thirties or early forties, that's an advanced age in this profession and time to slow down, so you need to think ahead. If you've done a range of theatrical, dance and acrobatic training, it'll be easier to redirect your career. You could create your own show, or teach, for example.

Interviewer: But once you become a trapeze artist, how do you get to be one of the best?

Jennie Thorpe: It's very competitive. All the trapeze artists I know are talented … and they're adaptable … and they're physically slim, which is necessary so your partner can catch you easily. But there's one quality only the best have, and it's a characteristic of real stars: they aren't at all nervous – when there are 5000 people watching them, they keep their cool, which is difficult, even if you know there's a safety net below to catch you if something goes wrong.

Interviewer: What do you love about your job and what's tough about it?

Jennie Thorpe: It's a physical challenge, but it's also an art. You're expressing yourself through the way you move. Working late each day, sometimes you wake up feeling you really want to stay in bed, but you still have to perform. I have rough hands from holding on to the trapeze bar, and sometimes they're painful, but they don't bother me as much as my sore muscles. That's something that never goes, really. I like to have a massage once a week.

Interviewer: But it is possible to learn circus skills just as a kind of exercise, isn't it?

Jennie Thorpe: Oh, yes, performing circus skills is great exercise in itself and has other benefits. I know there are schools where they've noticed an improvement in the schoolwork of students with concentration problems as a result of learning circus skills, because it helps them focus on one thing. They all start at the same point, discovering their own strengths and limitations in this new area, and it's fun!

Interviewer: So what does the future hold for you, Jennie?

Jennie Thorpe: I've been looking at the possibility of doing a part-time course and getting a management qualification at college, with a view to starting my own circus school when my contract with the circus runs out in two years' time. That'll only be possible if the circus manager allows me the time off, so we'll see.

Interviewer: Jennie, many thanks.

First Certificate Examination: Top 20 Questions

1 How many marks are needed to pass the exam?

➤ To pass the exam with a grade C, you need around 60% of the total marks.

2 Do I have to pass each paper in order to pass the exam?

➤ No. Each paper doesn't have a pass or fail mark. The final grade, A, B, C, D or E is arrived at by adding the weighted marks from all the papers together.

3 Are marks deducted for wrong answers?

➤ No. If you're not sure, make a guess, you may be right.

4 Am I allowed to use a dictionary?

No.

5 In Paper 1 (Reading), Part 3 has more questions, so is it more important?

➤ No. The three parts are equally weighted. In Parts 1 and 2, each question = 2 marks, whereas in Part 3, each question = 1 mark.

6 In Paper 1 (Reading), how long should I take on each question?

➤ This is up to you. You can do the tasks in any order and knowing how to use your time well is part of the test.

7 In Paper 2 (Writing), what happens if I don't use all the information given in Part 1?

➤ You will lose marks. The examiners are looking for both correct information and good language. So read the question, the input text and the handwritten notes very carefully.

8 In Paper 2 (Writing), how should I lay out the addresses?

➤ Don't include the addresses. If you do include them, the examiners will ignore them, as this is not part of the task.

9 In Paper 2 (Writing), what happens if I write too many or too few words?

➤ The word count is given as a guide only. Don't waste time counting; the examiners don't, they are more interested in your English! It is unlikely that answers under 120 words will contain enough information/ideas to fulfil the task. Overlong answers are more likely to contain mistakes. Plan your time so that you write about the right amount and have time to check what you have written.

10 In Paper 3 (Use of English), what happens if I get the right answer, but make a small mistake in a key word transformation?

➤ There are 2 marks for each answer, so you could still get 1 mark even if there was a small error.

11 In Paper 3 (Use of English), Parts 2, 3 and 4, if I am not sure, can I give two alternative answers?

➤ If there are two answers, and one of them is wrong, no marks are given. So, it's better to decide which of your answers is best!

12 In Paper 3 (Use of English), Parts 2 and 3, do contractions count as one word or two?

➤ Two, e.g. *don't* = two words, *do* + *not*.

13 What happens if I misspell a word in Paper 3 (Use of English), Parts 2, 3 and 4?

➤ All spelling must be correct in Paper 3.

14 What happens if I misspell a word in Paper 4 (Listening)?

➤ As long as the word is recognisable, you will get a mark. Spelling is not tested in Paper 4.

15 How many times will I hear each recording in Paper 4 (Listening)?

➤ Each text is played twice.

16 In Paper 4 (Listening), Part 2, do I have to use the words in the recording or other words?

➤ The word(s) you need to write are heard in the recording and are heard in the same order as the questions.

17 In Paper 4 (Listening), Part 2, what happens if my answer is too long to fit on the answer sheet?

➤ Most answers are single words, numbers or groups of 2–3 words. If you think the answer is longer, then it is probably the wrong answer. If you write information which is not the answer in addition to the answer, you will not get the mark, as you have not shown that you know exactly what the answer is.

18 In Paper 5 (Speaking), do I have to go with another student? Can I choose my partner?

➤ You cannot be examined alone as the ability to discuss with another student is being tested in Part 3. In some centres you can choose your partner, in others not. You should ask the local organiser. Don't forget that in Parts 1, 2 and 4 of the test, you talk to the examiner, not to your partner.

19 In Paper 5 (Speaking), is it a good idea to prepare what you are going to say in Part 1?

➤ It's a good idea to practise, but don't forget that the examiners give marks for natural communication in English. If you give a prepared speech which doesn't answer the examiner's question, you will lose marks.

20 In Paper 5 (Speaking), what if my partner makes lots of mistakes, or doesn't talk in Part 3?

➤ Don't worry. The examiners will help if necessary. Don't forget, you are not in competition with your partner. If you can help them, this will impress the examiners. Remember that Part 3 is about interaction, so you have to ask and answer questions as well as say what you think.

UNIVERSITY *of* CAMBRIDGE
ESOL Examinations

Do not write in this box

Candidate Name
If not already printed, write name
in CAPITALS and complete the
Candidate No. grid (in pencil).

Candidate Signature

SAMPLE

Examination Title

Centre

Supervisor:
If the candidate is ABSENT or has WITHDRAWN shade here ▭

Centre No.

Candidate No.

Examination Details

0	0	0	0
1	1	1	1
2	2	2	2
3	3	3	3
4	4	4	4
5	5	5	5
6	6	6	6
7	7	7	7
8	8	8	8
9	9	9	9

Candidate Answer Sheet

Instructions

Use a PENCIL (B or HB).

Mark ONE letter for each question.

For example, if you think B is the right answer to the question, mark your answer sheet like this:

| 0 | A B C D E F G H |

Rub out any answer you wish to change using an eraser.

1	A B C D E F G H
2	A B C D E F G H
3	A B C D E F G H
4	A B C D E F G H
5	A B C D E F G H
6	A B C D E F G H
7	A B C D E F G H
8	A B C D E F G H
9	A B C D E F G H
10	A B C D E F G H
11	A B C D E F G H
12	A B C D E F G H
13	A B C D E F G H
14	A B C D E F G H
15	A B C D E F G H
16	A B C D E F G H
17	A B C D E F G H
18	A B C D E F G H
19	A B C D E F G H
20	A B C D E F G H

21	A B C D E F G H
22	A B C D E F G H
23	A B C D E F G H
24	A B C D E F G H
25	A B C D E F G H
26	A B C D E F G H
27	A B C D E F G H
28	A B C D E F G H
29	A B C D E F G H
30	A B C D E F G H
31	A B C D E F G H
32	A B C D E F G H
33	A B C D E F G H
34	A B C D E F G H
35	A B C D E F G H
36	A B C D E F G H
37	A B C D E F G H
38	A B C D E F G H
39	A B C D E F G H
40	A B C D E F G H

A-H 40 CAS

denote Print Limited 0121 520 5100

DP594/300

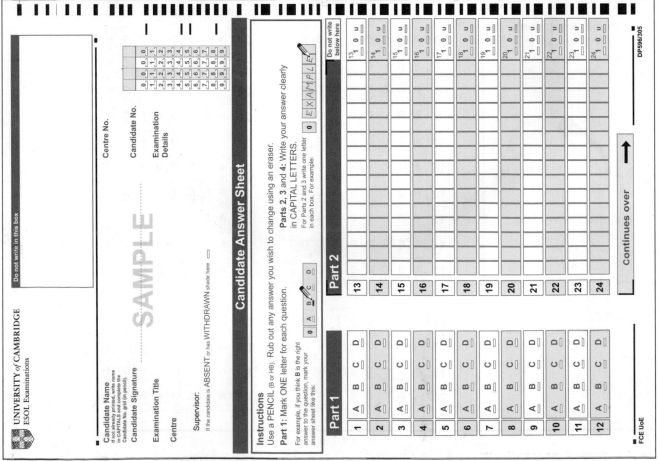

Part 3

SAMPLE

Part 3: 25, 26, 27, 28, 29, 30, 31, 32, 33, 34

Part 4

SAMPLE

Part 4: 35, 36, 37, 38, 39, 40, 41, 42

denote Print Limited 0121 520 5100

UNIVERSITY *of* CAMBRIDGE
ESOL Examinations

Do not write in this box

SAMPLE

Candidate Name
If not already printed, write name
in CAPITALS and complete the
Candidate No. grid (in pencil).

Candidate Signature

Examination Title

Centre

Supervisor:
If the candidate is ABSENT or has WITHDRAWN shade here

Centre No.

Candidate No.

Examination
Details

Candidate Answer Sheet

Instructions
Use a PENCIL (B or HB). Rub out any answer you wish to change using an eraser.

Part 1: Mark ONE letter for each question.

For example, if you think **B** is the right
answer to the question, mark your
answer sheet like this:

0 A B C D

Parts 2, 3 and 4: Write your answer clearly
in CAPITAL LETTERS.

For Parts 2 and 3 write one letter
in each box. For example:

0 EXAMPLE

Part 1

1 A B C D
2 A B C D
3 A B C D
4 A B C D
5 A B C D
6 A B C D
7 A B C D
8 A B C D
9 A B C D
10 A B C D
11 A B C D
12 A B C D

Part 2

13, 14, 15, 16, 17, 18, 19, 20, 21, 22, 23, 24

Continues over

FCE UoE

DP596/305